At the Table

A Luscious Collection of Philadelphia's Favorite Recipes

From the Women's Board of Thomas Jefferson University Hospital, Philadelphia, PA

At the Table

WOMEN'S BOARD OF THOMAS JEFFERSON UNIVERSITY HOSPITAL

WIMMER
cookbooks
A CONSOLIDATED GRAPHICS COMPANY
wimmerco.com   800.548.2537

Table of Contents

Message from the
TJUH Women's Board President

Welcome Jefferson cooks! The Thomas Jefferson University Hospital Women's Board is proud to offer: *At The Table — A Luscious Collection of Philadelphia's Favorite Recipes*, to our friends, families, colleagues, and supporters of the Jefferson community. We have baked, boiled, basted, browned, broiled, grilled, sautéed, mashed, mixed, puréed and whipped our way through hundreds of recipes in order to select our favorites for your culinary pleasure. *At The Table* brings together traditional Philadelphia recipes and adopted favorites with a Philadelphia twist.

Beginning in 1892, when a small cadre of Philadelphia women was encouraged to form a Women's Auxiliary at the Jefferson Medical College, their mission has always been clear and unwavering — to provide for the comfort and care of hospitalized persons. This devoted group of women was the predecessor of the present day Women's Board of the Thomas Jefferson University Hospital. The Women's Board has supported the Hospital's mission for over one hundred years through volunteer hours and fund-raising activities.

With *At The Table*, our most ambitious project to date, we continue the Thomas Jefferson University Hospital Women's Board tradition of bringing forth a quality product and our top performance. A special note of gratitude to Co-Chairs, Sharyn Vergare and Ann Pereira-Ogan for their tireless efforts and professionalism in bringing forth this project. Way to go gals! We hope that you will enjoy preparing and sampling the fabulous recipes offered herein and thank you so much for your support of this distinctive project.

Best wishes always,

Theresa Pluth Yeo

President, Women's Board, Thomas Jefferson University Hospital
Philadelphia, PA

Greeting from Thomas Jefferson University Hospital President

For more than a century, the Women's Board of Thomas Jefferson University Hospitals has served as a driving force behind the growth of patient care programs and resources across our community. Its dedicated members have raised millions of dollars to support Jefferson's goals of ensuring patient comfort and redefining clinical care, touching nearly every segment of our population along the way.

The legacy of the Women's Board is alive and evident everyday in many places throughout the hospital. They have generously supported facility upgrades to better accommodate the needs of our patients and their families, funded programs such as the expanding social work emergency fund designed to support patients in need of ongoing support as they transition to a non-acute care setting, and providing funding to enhance programs that touch all of our patients such as the pastoral care program. With *At The Table — A Luscious Collection of Philadelphia's Favorite Recipes*, these women are continuing their mission of raising funds dedicated to the care and comfort of our patients. I hope you enjoy exploring the many delicious recipes on the pages that follow.

Contributions from the Women's Board are especially meaningful to everyone at Jefferson because we know how much time and effort the entire board gives to its fundraising endeavors. Through your purchase of this cookbook, you too will be helping us offer programs that ensure better experiences for our patients. Thank you to all who have played a role in supporting this special project.

Sincerely,

Thomas J. Lewis

President and Chief Executive Officer
Thomas Jefferson University Hospital
Philadelphia, PA

At The Table Cookbook Committee

CO-CHAIRS and CO-EDITORS: Sharyn Vergare, Theresa Pluth Yeo
and Ann Pereira-Ogan

SECTION CHAIRS	COMMITTEE MEMBERS
Antonia Muskett Caruso	Ingrid Butcher
Mary Anne Fellman	Linda Hunt
Susan Horwitz Goldberg	Kathleen Fox
Drucie Isenberg	Hava Grunwald
Tae-ock Kauh	Cheryl Atkins-Lubinski
Nancy Kiss	Therese McDevitt
Audrey Knowles	Robin Williams
Carol Levin	Historical Vignettes: Theresa Pluth Yeo and Vanessa Weisman
Joanne Marshall	
Rosemary McNulty	Food Photographer: Jim Graham
Elinor Medoff	Food Stylist: Maria J. Soriano
Claudia Nazarian	Art Direction and Design: Barry Smith, Art Director
Sharyn Vergare	Thomas Jefferson University Hospital
Theresa Pluth Yeo	

Cookbook Sponsors

GOLD ($5,000 - $9,999)

Mrs. Vivian Farber

Mrs. Dorrance Hamilton

The Maternity Department of the Women's Board

The Martha Jefferson Department of the Women's Board

Thomas Jefferson University

SILVER ($1,000 - $4,999)

Thomas & Rosemary Costello

The Hamilton Family Foundation

Mr. Thomas Lewis

Joseph & Anita Majdan

Michael & Sharyn Vergare

Charles & Theresa Yeo

BRONZE ($500 - $999)

Levon & Claudia Nazarian

Caro Rock

FRIEND ($100 - $499)

Cheryl Atkins-Lubinski	Zvi & Hava Grunwald	John & Kathleen McCoy
Ingrid Butcher	Mrs. Eugene Jaeger	John & Rosemary McNulty
John W. & Antonia Caruso	Jonathon James	John & Joanne Marshall
Mrs. Natalie Cohn	Mrs. Ellen Judy	Packer Avenue Foods
Mrs. Jerome Cotler	Dr. Hyman Kahn	Miriam Schwartz
Harriet Disston	Dr. Taeock Kauh	TD Bank
Mary Anne Fellman	Audrey Knowles	Vanessa Weisman
Susan & Sherwood "Woody" Goldberg	Mrs. Emanuel Landau	Robin Williams
	Carol Levin	

Recipe Contributors and Testers

Toni Agnes
Nancy Armstrong
Cheryl Atkins-Lubinski
Rachel Behrendt
Kate Beishline
Dorothy Binswanger
Alice Blatner
Janet Blenheim
Jacqueline Borden
Bernadette Brescia
Kathleen Brescia
Joan Brucker
Ingrid Butcher
Sherry Burrell
Barbara Cahill
Antonia Muskett Caruso
John W. Caruso
Julie Chelius
Julieanne Cody
Virginia Coburn
Rhona Cohen
Linda Colombani
Seena Copeland
Jeanne Abruzzo DeSantis
Annette DiPietrae
Harriet Disston
Jane Dorey
Nancy Eid
Christina Edwards
Rebecca Edwards-Ronning
Meg Feehan
Mary Anne Fellman
Carol Ferguson
Marlene Brenner Ferguson
Toniann Flanigan
Brian Forbes
Jack Francis Catering
Dorothea Frederick
Cheryl Johnson Harnden
Rebecca Heider

Lynne Henningsen
Carol Hershkowitz
Pat Hirsekorn
Jean Hofmann
Liz Hosey
Linda Hunt
Eleanor Gates
Bethany Gindhart
Annette Dipietrae Girard
Amy Girardi
Susan Horwitz Goldberg
Clara Callahan Goodman
Hava Grunwald
Drucie Isenberg
Henrietta Jaeger
Jon Jividen (12th Street Catering)
Mary K. Joseph
Judy Juzaitis
Taeock Kauh
Audrey Knowles
Vivian Koo
Amy Koniers
Mollie Koniers
Cathy Kramer
Lynn Krensel & Salvo Cucino
Lorraine Lerner
Cheryl Lillemoe
Ellen Lindner
Debbie Lofton
Joanne McCollum
Kathleen McCoy
Therese McDevitt
Cheryl McEvoy
Kimberly McGehee
Nicolette McGlashan
Eileen McGowan
Christine McLean
Dan & Kim McNulty
Jackie McNulty
Rosemary McNulty

Teri Manning
Maria Marinelli
Joanne Marshall
Lisa Marzucco
Janice May
Charlotte Merli
Jennifer Miller
Melissa Morris
Kitty Moses
Frances Mueller
JoAnn Mueller
Donna Muizelaar
Susan Murphy
Linda Mutch
Anne Mutch
Lori Nagler
National Foundation
    for Celiac Awareness
Claudia Nazarian
Ann Pereira-Ogan
Ric Orlando
Rebecca O'Shea
Megan Vergare Ostuni
Anna O'Toole
Laura Patarcity
Terri Peters
Ann Phalen
Maria Pickering
Elizabeth Pitt
Meg Pluth
Rudy Pluth
Margaret Pluth
Selina Poiesz
Ruth Pomerantz
Coleen Pontin
Stephanie Pontin
Kelly Purvis
Vijay Rao
Helaine Ridilla
Roberto's Ristoranti c/o Bob Caruso
Jean Robertson
Mary Robertson
Caro Rock

Alice Romanelli
Marie Romanelli
Jeannette Rosato
Melissa Ross
Pam Schlichter
Miriam Schwartz
Elizabeth Vergare Shane
Ryan Shane
Edna Shaw
Margaret Siegfeldt
Donna Smith
Jonne Smith
Kellie Smith
Sylvia Smith
Thelma Snyder
Marilyn Sprague
Walter Staib
Maggie Sturgis
Erica & Emily Swan
Alice Lea Tasman
The Prime Rib
Gerri Toscano
Joanne Treadway
Jacqueline Trojen
Judith Tykocinski
Nancy Urbanski
Gloria Uremevich
Julia Ward
Virginia Waters
Rich Webster
Kathleen Wilson
Matthew Vergare
Mary Vergare
Michael Vergare
Sharyn Vergare
Patricia Murtaugh Wagner
Vanessa Weisman
Robin Williams
Charles Yeo
Katerina Yeo
Theresa Pluth Yeo
Mary Hanson-Zalot

The Thomas Jefferson University Hospital Women's Board and Hospital President Thomas J. Lewis at the unveiling of the Women's Board Dedication Wall, June 2012. www.jeffersonhospital.org/womensboard/

Breakfast & Breads

Zucchini Bread, recipe page 13

1824 – Jefferson Medical College

Philadelphia, PA

Zucchini Bread *(pictured)*

2 LOAVES

3	eggs	3	cups flour
1	cup brown sugar, packed	1	teaspoon salt
1	cup sugar	½	teaspoon cinnamon
1	cup oil	1	teaspoon baking powder
2	cups zucchini, grated	1	teaspoon baking soda
1	teaspoon vanilla		confectioners' sugar

In a large bowl, beat eggs until frothy. Stir in brown sugar, sugar, oil, zucchini and vanilla. In a separate bowl, combine dry ingredients, reserving confectioners' sugar, then stir into the zucchini mixture until well mixed. Pour batter into 2 well greased loaf pans. Bake at 325° for 1 hour or until well done. Slightly cool in pans, remove from pans and cool completely before slicing. Dust with confectioners' sugar if desired.

Uncle Jack's Foolproof Biscuits

12 BISCUITS

Very easy, light and foolproof!

2	cups biscuit baking mix	½	cup softened butter
½	cup cold water		

Mix all ingredients with pastry blender or 2 forks until soft dough forms. Beat vigorously for 20 strokes. Form into biscuits and drop onto greased cookie sheet. Bake at 400° for 8 to 10 minutes until edges are medium brown.

Uncle Jack was former Women's Board President's Sharyn Vergare's uncle.
He served as a navy cook during World War II and these biscuits are still foolproof today!

1680

Sticky buns are a Philadelphia specialty. They probably descended from German "Schnecken", similar to cinnamon rolls. The recipe for Schnecken ("snails") was brought to Philadelphia by Germans who settled in the Germantown section in the early 1680s.

Sweet Potato and Pecan Biscuits

MAKES ABOUT 2 DOZEN BISCUITS

This biscuit dough freezes beautifully unbaked. Just layer the dough between wax paper and store for up to 3 months. Defrost the dough and follow baking directions. It pays to make a double batch of these biscuits and freeze half for later.

5	cups all-purpose flour
1	cup light brown sugar, packed
2	tablespoons baking powder
1½	teaspoons ground cinnamon
1	teaspoon salt
1	teaspoon ground ginger
½	teaspoon ground allspice
1	cup vegetable shortening
2	cups cooked, mashed and cooled sweet potatoes (about 2 large potatoes)
1	cup heavy cream
½	cup coarsely chopped pecans

Preheat oven to 400°. In a large mixing bowl, mix together flour, brown sugar, baking powder, cinnamon, salt, ginger and allspice. Add the shortening, and cut in with a pastry cutter or two knives until crumbly. Stir in the sweet potato. Add the cream and pecans, and stir until just moistened. Turn the dough out into a lightly-floured work surface. Roll the dough out to 1½ inches thick, and cut out biscuits with a floured 2 inch biscuit cutter. Place biscuits 1 inch apart on ungreased baking pans. Set pans in the oven; reduce oven temperature to 350°, and bake for 25 to 30 minutes, or until golden brown. Serve warm or cool completely on a wire rack.

In the 18th century, sweet potatoes were plentiful in the southern states, and Thomas Jefferson participated as enthusiastically in their cultivation as other farmers. George Washington, in fact, was one of his compatriots in this venture. This root vegetable makes a number of appearances in Jefferson's collection of recipes and, consequently, inspired this recipe. Sweet potatoes contribute a sweet flavor and light texture to these biscuits and are complemented by the addition of one of this renowned gardener's other favorite foods, pecans.

Breakfast & Breads

Reprinted with permission from *The City Tavern Cookbook: Recipes from the Birthplace of American Cuisine* ©2009 by Walter Staib.

Irish Soda Bread

2 LOAVES

5¼	cups all-purpose flour	2	cups buttermilk
1	cup sugar	3	tablespoons unsalted butter, melted
1½	tablespoons baking powder		
1½	teaspoons salt	3	eggs, beaten
1¾	cups golden raisins	2	tablespoons sugar
1¼	teaspoons caraway seeds		

In a large mixing bowl, sift and mix dry ingredients. Add raisins and caraway seeds. In another large mixing bowl, mix buttermilk, butter and eggs. Add dry ingredients to wet mixture and stir to combine. Turn into greased bread pans or round cake pans. Sprinkle sugar on top of loaves. Bake at 375° for 10 minutes, then reduce heat to 350° and bake for 45 minutes. Cool on rack.

Jean's Blueberry Cake

8-10 SERVINGS

½	cup butter	½	teaspoon salt
¾	cup granulated sugar	2	cups blueberries, well drained
1	egg	¼	cup butter
½	cup milk	⅓	cup flour
2	cups flour	½	cup sugar
2	teaspoons baking powder	½	teaspoon cinnamon

Mix together the butter, sugar and egg. Sift and add flour, baking powder and salt. Add blueberries. Spread batter in 9x12-inch baking pan. Cut butter, flour, sugar and cinnamon together until crumbs form. Spread on top of batter. Bake 45 to 50 minutes at 350°.

1824

The Jefferson Medical College was founded in Center City, Philadelphia, PA under the direction of Dr. George McClellan, Dr. Joseph Klapp, Dr. John Eberle and Mr. Jacob Green. It was the second medical school in the city and the Tivoli Theater on Prune Street was its first home.

1682

The Blue Anchor Tavern was the first tavern in Philadelphia and was imported, prefabricated, from England in October 1682 at the present 242-244 South Front Street. It remained open until 1810. Although the Blue Anchor was a fish house, it also served dishes such as wild pigeon, shad, sturgeon, and salt oysters in season. A whortleberry swamp was located nearby which allowed the tavern to also offer whortleberry pie.

Sweet Breakfast Braided Bread   3 LOAVES

Goes well with a meal, toasted for breakfast or to make French toast.

2	packages yeast	1	teaspoon vanilla
1½	cups water	7½-8	cups all-purpose flour
2	tablespoons granulated sugar	½	teaspoon salt
1	stick butter	¾	cup sugar
3	eggs (plus 1 for glaze)		

In a small mixing bowl, dissolve 2 packages of yeast in warm water (100-110°) and stir in 2 tablespoons granulated sugar (this will get bubbly and rise). Melt butter and let cool slightly. Beat 3 eggs in a small mixing bowl and add vanilla. While the yeast rises and butter cools, in a large bowl mix flour, salt and sugar. Make a well in the center and add yeast, butter and beaten eggs. With wooden spoon, stir from center, adding more of the surrounding flour with each turn to obtain rough dough (should be sticky). Transfer to a floured surface and knead until smooth and elastic (about 10 minutes). Place in a clean, greased bowl, cover and leave to rise in a warm place until dough doubles (about 1 ½ hours). Grease 2 baking sheets. Punch dough down and divide into 9 equal pieces. Roll each piece into a strip about 12 inches long. Braid strips together and pinch ends. Cover and let rise for 1½ hours – don't over rise. Brush tops with beaten egg. Preheat oven to 375° for 15 minutes. Bake at 375° for 30 minutes or until golden brown. Set on rack to cool completely.

Aunt Katherine's German Sour Cream Coffee Cake

A delicious coffee cake; nice for family gatherings.

CAKE

1½	sticks butter
2	cups sugar
4	large eggs at room temperature
1	teaspoon vanilla extract

3	cups flour
2	teaspoons baking soda
1	pint sour cream

TOPPING

1	stick butter
⅓	cup brown sugar

⅔	cup white sugar
¾	cup flour

Cake: In a large mixing bowl, cream butter and sugar until light. Add eggs, one at a time, beating well after each addition. Add vanilla. In a separate bowl, sift together flour and baking soda. Gradually add flour mixture until combined. Fold in sour cream. Topping: In a small bowl, combine topping ingredients. Using a pastry cutter or 2 knives, cut ingredients to form coarse crumbs (don't over mix). To assemble: Preheat oven to 375°. Pour batter into a greased 10x14-inch baking pan (lasagna pan); sprinkle crumb mixture over top of cake. Bake for 12 minutes, reduce heat to 350° and bake for another 15 minutes or until crumbs are brown. Cool slightly. Cut into pieces to serve.

1872

The Kraft company records place the invention of cream cheese in the hands of a New York dairyman named William A. Lawrence, who first experimented with milk and cream in 1872. It was called the Star Brand. The name "Philadelphia" was adopted for the product because the Pennsylvania city was treasured as the seat of high-quality foods, particularly dairy products.

1831

Dr. John Revere, grandson of revolutionary patriot, Paul Revere, received his medical degree from the University of Edinburgh and was a Jefferson Professor of Medicine and the Dean of the Medical College until 1841.

Roasted Shrimp Benedict with Orange and Caper Sauce

4 SERVINGS

12	large shrimp, peeled and uncooked
1	tablespoon olive oil
	salt
	pepper
	orange zest
1	tablespoon cider vinegar
3	tablespoons fresh orange juice
½	cup mayonnaise
2	tablespoons capers
¼	cup dill, chopped
4	eggs, poached or soft boiled
2	English muffins

Place shrimp on a roasting pan and coat with oil, salt and pepper. Roast at 400° until pink. In a mixing bowl, combine vinegar, mayonnaise, orange juice, orange zest, capers and dill. Whisk together. Poach or soft boil eggs. Toast English muffins. Assemble with 3 shrimp on each half of muffin, then 1 egg on each half and drizzle with sauce.

Substitute cornbread for English muffins.

Blintz Casserole

Top with fresh fruit or blueberry or cherry pie filling.

12	frozen cheese blintzes
¼	stick butter
¼	cup sugar
1	pint sour cream
6	eggs
1½	teaspoons vanilla
¼	cup orange juice
	cinnamon, to garnish

Preheat oven to 350°. Melt butter in a 9x13-inch ovenproof dish. Lay frozen blintzes on top of butter. Combine other ingredients (except cinnamon) and pour over blintzes. Sprinkle cinnamon on top. Bake 45 minutes.

Overnight French Toast Casserole

Great for brunches or holiday morning breakfast. Always a family favorite.

1	cup light brown sugar	1	loaf French bread	
½	cup melted unsalted butter, melted	6	eggs	
2	tablespoons light corn syrup	2	cups milk	
1	dash nutmeg	1½	teaspoons vanilla	
½	teaspoon cinnamon	2	teaspoons (or more) cinnamon sugar	

Combine first 5 ingredients. Pour into a greased 9x13-inch pan (glass pan is best). Slice bread into ½ inch to ¾ inch thick rounds. Beat eggs, milk and vanilla by hand until blended and pour over bread. Sprinkle with cinnamon sugar. Cover and refrigerate overnight. Bake uncovered for 30 to 35 minutes at 325°.

Early Morning Delight

6-8 SERVINGS

6-8	slices bread, torn	8	eggs	
1	pound bulk sausage, browned and drained	2	cups milk	
1	cup sharp Cheddar cheese, grated	1	teaspoon dry mustard	
		1	teaspoon pepper	
		1	teaspoon salt	

Layer bread, followed by sausage, then cheese in a 9x13-inch greased pan. Mix eggs, milk, mustard, salt and pepper in a blender. Pour over the bread mix. Refrigerate overnight. Bake uncovered at 350° for 45 minutes.

In place of sausage, may use a mixture of sautéed onions, tomatoes and peppers.

1839

Austrian Francis Grund wrote in his 1839 book, <u>Aristocracy in America</u>: *"The New Englanders are an arguing people, and annoy you, even in society, with mathematical and political demonstrations. The Philadelphians have more taste, and have the best cooks in the United States."*

1858

*John Landis Mason,
a Philadelphia tinsmith,
patented the Mason
jar in 1858.*

Quick Eggs Benedict

4 SERVINGS

4	slices Canadian bacon		1	dash ground cayenne pepper
1	teaspoon white vinegar		¼	teaspoon salt
4	whole eggs		1	tablespoon lemon juice
1	cup butter		4	English muffins, split and toasted
3	egg yolks			
1	tablespoon heavy cream			

Fry the Canadian bacon on both sides, until evenly browned. Fill a large saucepan with 3 to 4 inches water, and bring to a simmer; then add the vinegar. Break the 4 whole eggs into the simmering water, and cook for 2 to 3 minutes. The whites should look set but the yolks should be still soft. Remove eggs with a slotted spoon and place to the side on a covered plate. Melt the butter until bubbly in a small pan or microwave; do not allow butter to brown. In a blender or large food processor, blend the 3 egg yolks, heavy cream, cayenne pepper, and salt until smooth. Pour half of the hot butter into the yolk mixture in a slow, thin steady stream. Should blend in as you are pouring it in. Blend in the lemon juice in the same way, then the remaining melted butter. Place the English muffins face up on plates. Top each muffin with 1 slice of Canadian bacon and 1 poached egg. Drizzle with the cream sauce, and serve immediately.

Mattie's Bran Muffins

12 MUFFINS

1	cup all-bran cereal		1	cup sifted flour
¾	cup milk		2½	teaspoons baking powder
1	egg		½	teaspoon salt
¼	cup shortening		¼	cup sugar

Combine bran cereal and milk- let mixture stand tell until moisture is nearly gone. Add egg and shortening, beat well. Sift together the flour, baking powder, salt and sugar. Add to first mixture and mix only until combined. Fill greased muffin tins ⅔ full. Bake at 400° for 30 minutes.

Cape Charles Omelette

4 SERVINGS

SAUCE

4	tablespoons butter	½	teaspoon thyme
4	tablespoons flour	1	teaspoon tamari
2	cups milk	1	teaspoon Worcestershire sauce

FILLING

3	tablespoons butter	½	teaspoon tarragon
½	pound crabmeat, cleaned		

OMELETTE

4   eggs, beaten

Sauce: Melt 4 tablespoons butter and add flour. Simmer. Add milk, thyme, tamari and Worcestershire; heat mixture, stirring until thick. Filling: In a separate saucepan, melt 3 tablespoons butter. Add crabmeat and tarragon. Stir until mixed. Add 1 cup of sauce to mixture. Omelette: Pour beaten eggs into heated omelet pan, let cook until edges are firm. Spread filling mixture across top of open omelette. Heat until omelette edges are slightly brown and warm throughout. Top omelette with remaining sauce. Cut into 4 pieces and serve hot.

Northern Baked Cheese Grits

6-8 SERVINGS

2	eggs, beaten	1	clove garlic, minced
¾	cup sharp Cheddar cheese, grated	2½	cups quick grits, cooked
2	teaspoons dry mustard	2	tablespoons butter or margarine for casserole dish
½	teaspoon salt		paprika

Mix eggs, cheese, mustard, salt and garlic. Stir into warm grits and pour into well buttered casserole dish. Bake at 350° for 50 minutes. Garnish with paprika.

Serve immediately.

1907-1931

John Chalmers DaCosta, MD, the Co-Chair of Surgery at Jefferson was responsible for the restoration of the "Old Operating Table", a walnut operating table which was constructed in America between the years 1850-1855 by an unknown manufacturer. The "OR" table is now located in the entranceway of the main surgery offices at Jefferson.

Granola

Great hostess gift!

1	pound rolled oats	½	teaspoon freshly grated nutmeg
1	cup slivered, blanched almonds	½	pound unsalted butter, cut into pieces
1	cup walnuts		
1	cup chopped pecans	⅓	cup pure maple syrup
½	cup brown sugar	¾	pound coarsely chopped raisins and dried cranberries
1	tablespoon chopped orange zest		
1	teaspoon ground cinnamon		

Preheat oven to 325°. Lightly butter 2 (12x17-inch) baking pans. Fit paddle onto electric mixer and on the lowest speed, combine oats, almonds, walnuts, pecans, sugar, orange zest, cinnamon and nutmeg. Mix for 1 minute. In a small saucepan, melt butter with maple syrup. Pour into the oat mixture and mix until just absorbed. Scrape into one of the prepared pans, spread and pat down evenly over the entire pan, making a layer that is about ½ inch thick. Bake 50 minutes, until golden brown. To invert, remove pan from the oven, lay the second pan over to fit exactly and turn. Scrape off any particles that stick to the first pan and pat back down on the layer of granola. (Don't break the granola apart until it is cool.) Return to oven and continue baking until the granola is golden brown and sticks together. Do not overbake. Remove from oven and cool completely. Transfer using thick baking mitts, as it will be very hot! Break into chunks in a large bowl and stir in the dried fruit, distributing them as evenly as you can through the granola. Store in a large airtight container.

Baked Apple Pecan Pancake

4-6 SERVINGS

¾ cup buttermilk pancake mix
½ cup milk
3 eggs
⅓ cup sugar

2 large tart cooking apples, sliced thinly
¼ cup butter, melted
¼ cup pecans, chopped
1 teaspoon cinnamon

Preheat oven to 450°. Combine pancake mix, milk, eggs and 1 teaspoon sugar, mix well. Sauté apples in melted butter in a 9 or 10 inch ovenproof skillet until tender. Remove skillet from heat, spread apples in pan, and sprinkle with nuts. Pour batter evenly over apples and nuts. In a separate bowl, combine remaining sugar and cinnamon, sprinkle over batter. Cover skillet with lid or foil, bake at 450° for 12 to 14 minutes until pancake is puffed and sugar is melted. Loosen side of pancake from skillet. Cool slightly. Cut into wedges.

Don't Tell Pancakes

Serve with dollop of sour cream and raspberry preserves or fresh berries

2 eggs, separated
    (whip egg whites and set aside)
1 cup sour cream
1 cup buttermilk

1 teaspoon sugar
1 teaspoon baking powder
1 cup flour
1 tablespoon honey

Mix all ingredients together except egg whites. After mixing, gently fold in egg whites. Onto a griddle preheated to medium high, spoon batter. Heat pancakes until light golden brown on downside (little bubbles will form on the "up" side); flip pancakes and heat a few more minutes. Serve immediately.

1889-1907

William Williams Keen, MD, was known as the "Marshall" of American surgery and a pioneer of neurosurgery. He was America's first brain surgeon.

1922

Edmund Nacchio took his parent's soft pretzel recipe and started to bake them in large quantities combining hand twisted pretzels and applying conveyor systems of equipment imported from Germany that could be used for mass production and baking and thereby established Federal Pretzel Baking Company.

Schnecken

24-32 COOKIES

½	pound cream cheese	cinnamon
1	stick butter	sugar
2	cups flour	raisins
½	teaspoon salt	chocolate chips
1	egg yolk	chopped nuts
1	tablespoon sugar	seedless raspberry jam
	zest of 1 orange	

Mix the first 7 ingredients together, using an electric mixer. Divide mixture into four balls, about the size of a tennis ball. Refrigerate for at least 2 hours. Remove from refrigerator and let stand at room temperature for about 15 minutes before rolling out. Sprinkle cinnamon and sugar generously onto a pastry cloth. Sprinkle cinnamon sugar mixture on flattened ball. Roll out ball to 6 or 7 inches in diameter. Spread with a thin layer of raspberry jam. Sprinkle chocolate chips or raisins or nuts. Divide into 6 to 8 triangular portions. Roll up each slice from wide side to point and place on a cookie sheet. Bake at 350° for 20 to 25 minutes. Cool and serve.

Gertrude's Creamy Cheesy Pancakes

12 PANCAKES

½	pound dry cottage cheese	¾	cup flour
½	cup sour cream	⅛	teaspoon baking powder
3	eggs lightly beaten		salt
¼	cup golden raisins (optional)		

Blend cheese and sour cream. Add eggs, raisins and salt. Sift dry ingredients together and add to batter. If batter is too thick, add a small amount of water. Line cookie sheet with parchment paper (lightly spray with oil to prevent sticking). Drop onto cookie sheet in heaping tablespoons. Bake at 400° for 40 minutes or until lightly brown on top.

This recipe is in memory of Gertrude Horwitz, who always cooked with heaping handfuls of love and happiness.

Potato Pancakes

4 SERVINGS

2	cups grated raw potatoes	¼	teaspoon baking powder
½	cup flour	2	tablespoons onion, grated (optional)
½	teaspoon salt	1	tablespoon vegetable oil
2	eggs		

Grate raw potatoes. Add all ingredients together in a large mixing bowl. Heat vegetable oil in a large skillet. Spoon dollops of batter into hot pan. Fry pancakes until golden brown, turning once. Serve with maple syrup and turkey sausage.

May use fresh chives in place of onion.

Breakfast Tostada

4 SERVINGS

Quickly prepared in a microwave oven.

¼	cup milk	1	cup canned black beans, rinse and drain
¼	teaspoon salt	½	cup salsa
⅛	teaspoon freshly ground black pepper	¼	cup fat-free sour cream
4	large egg whites	¼	cup guacamole
2	large whole eggs		parsley sprigs
4	(6-inch) corn tortillas		dash of paprika
½	cup shredded low-fat sharp Cheddar cheese or Monterey Jack cheese		

Combine milk, salt, pepper, egg whites and whole eggs in a large microwave-safe dish. Whisk together. Microwave on HIGH for 3 minutes. Place one tortilla each on a microwave safe plate. Divide egg mixture evenly among the 4 tortillas. Layer each tortilla with 2 tablespoons cheese, ¼ cup beans and 1 tablespoon green onions. Microwave each tortilla for 30 seconds. Top each tortilla with 2 tablespoons salsa, sour cream and guacamole. Garnish with parsley and sprinkle of paprika.

1875

Thomas Eakins painted the controversial "The Gross Clinic", which featured Dr. Samuel D. Gross performing an operation on a young lad. The Jefferson Medical College Class of 1877 later purchased the painting for $200 as a gift to the Medical College. It hung in McClellan Hall for many years and later in the Eakins Lounge before being sold jointly to the Philadelphia Museum of Art and Pennsylvania Academy of Fine Arts in 2006.

Cinnamon Buns

18 BUNS

2   loaves frozen bread dough (defrosted)
    raisins
½   cup white sugar
½   cup brown sugar

1   teaspoon cinnamon
½   box dry butterscotch instant pudding
1   stick butter

Use a lasagna pan. Grease pan with vegetable shortening and sprinkle bottom with as many raisins as you like. Cut dough into 18 sections and arrange in pan. Mix together sugars, cinnamon, and butterscotch pudding. Sprinkle mixture over dough. Place pan in cold oven overnight (dough will rise). Dot with butter. Bake at 350° for 30 minutes.

Enjoy these yummy buns fresh from the oven.

Biscottini Di Prato

An old recipe from the Stango family.

3   cups all-purpose flour
1¼ cups sugar
8   ounces almonds or filberts

1   teaspoon baking powder
    pinch of salt
1   stick (4 ounces) unsalted cold butter (cut into 1 inch pieces)

Preheat oven to 325° and grease 3 loaf pans generously with shortening. Coarsely chop nuts in blender or food processor and toast lightly. Thoroughly combine flour, sugar, nuts, baking powder and salt in a large mixing bowl. Cut in butter with a pastry blender until it resembles coarse crumbs. Add eggs and mix until barely combined. Do not overwork.
Divide dough into 3 equal portions. Pack tightly into greased pans. Bake at 325° for 30 minutes. Remove from oven and cut into ½ inch slices. Return to oven and bake for an additional 15 to 20 minutes. Remove from oven and remove from pans. Let cool on waxed paper. Store in airtight containers when cooled.

Great for dunking in coffee or tea.

Appetizers

Watermelon Feta Skewers, recipe page 33

1908 – The Diet Kitchen

Food has always been an important component of the health and welfare of Jefferson Medical College patients. The "diet kitchen" (circa 1908) prepared nutritious meals for patients at the Hospital.

1833

Jefferson Medical College graduate, Ninian Pickney, MD, returned to his native Maryland after graduation and later became the first Medical Director of the Navy (the title was later changed to Surgeon General).

Shrimp Mousse

2	cans medium shrimp, chopped in half	8	ounces cream cheese, softened
¾	cup onion, chopped	1	cup mayonnaise
¾	cup celery, chopped	1	packet unflavored gelatin
		1	can tomato soup

Heat soup (do not add milk or water) to a boil. Dissolve 2 tablespoons of the gelatin into hot soup. In another bowl mix onion, celery, cream cheese and mayonnaise. Add soup and mix. Gradually add shrimp. Pour into a 10 inch well-oiled ring mold and refrigerate. Invert on serving plate and serve with crackers.

Yummy Onion Spread

Use a sweet onion, (Vidalia or red).

1	cup Swiss cheese, grated	1	small can black olives, sliced
1	cup mayonnaise	2	ounces Parmesan cheese, plus extra for the top
1	onion, chopped thin		

Combine all ingredients. Put into a small casserole dish. Sprinkle with Parmesan cheese. Bake at 350° for 20 to 30 minutes. Serve with a cracker that isn't too salty.

Fresh Salsa

2	cups plum tomatoes, cored, seeded and chopped	1	medium onion, chopped
1½	teaspoons salt	1	cup roasted corn kernels (fresh, canned or frozen) or 1 can black beans
1	fresh jalapeño pepper, seeded and chopped		juice of 1 lime
2	red bell peppers, seeded and chopped	½	cup fresh cilantro, chopped
		1½	teaspoons toasted cumin

Toss all ingredients and let sit several hours before serving with tortilla chips.

As early as 1683, oysters — some of which were over a foot in length — were a major factor in attracting Europeans to move to the Colonies. The discarded shells were used as street paving, artificial wharves and ship ballast.

Baked Wontons with Crabmeat

2	tablespoons vegetable oil	⅓	teaspoon salt
1	medium chopped onion	¼	teaspoon black pepper
2	stalks chopped celery	40	square wonton wrappers
2	cups ground pork	¼	cup soy sauce
1	cup crabmeat	2	tablespoons rice vinegar

Heat oil in pan, then cook onion and celery until they begin to soften. Add pork to mixture, cook well. Set aside until cool. Mix cooled pork with crabmeat, parsley, salt and pepper. Place 1 tablespoon of filling in the center of each wrapper. Moisten the edges with water, then make a triangle shape and seal the edges. Place filled wontons in a muffin pan and bake at 350° oven for 30 minutes. Combine soy sauce and vinegar to make dipping sauce for wontons.

Party Bruschetta

2	large cloves garlic	¼	cup Parmesan cheese, shredded
½	teaspoon salt	2	tablespoons olive oil
3	cups tomato, finely chopped, seeds removed or 1 (28 ounce) can petite diced tomatoes well-drained	½	teaspoon sugar
		¼	teaspoon pepper
		8	ounces cream cheese
¼	cup pesto (prepared or use recipe on page 196)	1	baguette

Mash garlic and salt into a paste. Add tomatoes, pesto, Parmesan cheese, olive oil, sugar and pepper and mix. Slice baguette and lightly brush slices with olive oil and toast very lightly in the oven. Spread cream cheese on toasted bread slices, top with tomato mixture. Garnish with fresh herbs, such as parsley, rosemary, thyme or basil.

Hot Spinach Balls

1   (10 ounce) package chopped spinach

2½ cups herb stuffing mix

¾   cup butter, softened

4   eggs

¾   cup Parmesan cheese

1   large onion

salt, pepper, thyme, nutmeg to taste

Cook spinach according to package directions and press out water. Combine remaining ingredients with spinach and roll into bite sized balls. Place on greased cookie sheet. Bake at 350° for 20 minutes, remove at once. Place on a paper towel. Can be frozen after cooking — reheat at 400° until hot. These are great served with honey mustard for dipping.

Anne Marie's Cheese and Carrot Spread

1   cup shredded carrots

1   cup Parmesan cheese

1   cup mayonnaise

Mix all ingredients together and bake at 425° for 20 minutes in an oven-safe serving bowl. Garnish with parsley.

Best Ever Guacamole

½   cup scallions, chopped

1   clove garlic, minced

1   beefsteak tomato, chopped

½   teaspoon salt

2   avocados, coarsely chopped

1-2 teaspoons freshly squeezed lime juice

Mix scallions, garlic and tomato and sprinkle with salt. Chop avocados and mix with tomato mixture. Squirt lime juice and sprinkle with salt to taste.

1886

The Maternity Department of the Hospital opened under the direction of Dr. Edward Davis at 327 Pine Street. The Hospital Trustees recommended that a Board of Lady Managers be commenced to assist with oversight of the Maternity Department.

1737-1761

*John Bartram,
King George III's
Royal Botanist,
cultivated
sweet marjoram,
oregano, and winter
marjoram for the first
time in the Colonies.*

Avocado-Goat Cheese Tostadas

SERVES 4

2	avocados	1	teaspoon tarragon, minced
4	ounces goat cheese	1	teaspoon mint, minced
½	teaspoon garlic, minced	1	tablespoon red pepper, diced
1	teaspoon orange juice	1	tablespoon yellow pepper, diced
1	teaspoon basil, minced	8	fresh white or blue tortillas, cut into rounds and fried
1	teaspoon cilantro, minced		

Pulse everything in a food processor until creamy but not whipped. Spoon or pipe onto tortillas, garnish with peppers.

Buffalo Ranch Chicken Dip

1	pound chicken, thighs or breasts	8	ounces cream cheese, softened
1	cup hot sauce	8	ounces Cheddar cheese, shredded
8	ounces ranch dressing		

Broil chicken and hand shred into small pieces. Mix chicken, hot sauce, dressing and cream cheese. Cover with Cheddar cheese. Bake at 350° for 30 to 40 minutes. Will be spicy!

Baked Havarti Cheese

1	can crescent rolls	1	pound block Havarti cheese
4	tablespoons champagne mustard		

Unroll crescent rolls and seal perforations together to make a rectangle. Spread with mustard. Place Havarti on top and wrap crescent rolls around the cheese and seal. Place on a greased baking sheet. Bake at 350° until golden brown, about 20 minutes.

Watermelon Feta Skewers *(pictured)*

A festive looking and tasty appetizer.

watermelon, cut into chunks
feta cheese, cut into squares
olive oil

balsamic vinegar
olive tapenade

Arrange watermelon chunks on a platter. Place feta on top of each chunk. Place a dab of olive tapenade on top of feta. Drizzle with olive oil and small amount of balsamic vinegar. Place toothpick in each bite.

Gorgonzola may be substituted for feta.

Kalamata Olive Tapenade

2	cloves garlic	¼	cup extra virgin olive oil
2	sun-dried tomatoes		pepper, to taste
2	cups pitted Kalamata olives		

Chop garlic in food processor, adding olives, sun-dried tomatoes, olive oil and pepper. Blend well. Serve on either toasted French bread or crackers.

Brown Sugar Shrimp

2	pounds large shrimp, cooked and peeled	½	cup mayonnaise
1	pound raw bacon, cut in half	½	cup brown sugar
		½	cup cocktail sauce

Wrap shrimp in bacon, secure with toothpick. Bake or broil until bacon begins to brown. Mix mayonnaise, brown sugar and cocktail sauce until sugar is dissolved. Pour over cooked shrimp. Bake at 350° until sauce is hot. Serve warm.

1897

The Maternity Committee was officially named in 1897 and is the oldest continually functioning committee of the Women's Board. Its focus is the welfare of infants and mothers. They provided food, domestic services and a portion of the Head Nurse's salary for the Maternity Department.

1773

The City Tavern was completed in 1773 and was considered one of the most elegant buildings in Philadelphia, reflecting its status as the largest, most cosmopolitan city in British North America.

Chutney Cheese Ball

May be frozen.

8	ounces cream cheese, softened	1	teaspoon curry powder
½	cup chutney, minced	¼	teaspoon dry mustard
¼	cup sliced almonds		coconut

Mix all ingredients together, except coconut. Shape into a ball and roll into coconut, if desired. Refrigerate before serving.

Chick-Pea and Red Pepper Dip

Serve with tortilla chips or vegetables.

1	(16 ounce) can chick-peas, drained	½	teaspoon salt
1	(7 ounce) jar roasted sweet red peppers	¼	teaspoon pepper
½	cup non-fat sour cream	10	drops Tabasco™ sauce to taste
1	garlic clove, minced		Mexican seasoning to taste
			paprika

Place all ingredients in a large food processor, mix until well blended. Chill at least 2 hours before serving. Sprinkle top with paprika before serving.

Parmesan Chicken Wings

1	cup Parmesan cheese, grated	½	teaspoon pepper
2	tablespoons parsley, chopped	4	pounds chicken wings, split and discard tips
2	teaspoons paprika		
1	tablespoon oregano	½	cup butter, melted
1	teaspoon salt		

Combine Parmesan cheese, parsley, paprika, oregano, salt and pepper. Dip chicken wings in butter, then coat with dry ingredients. Place on cookie sheet. Bake at 350° for 1 hour.

Mushroom Hors D'oeuvres   6 SERVINGS

1	package crescent rolls	1	tablespoon Dijon mustard
1	(3 ounce) package cream cheese		dehydrated onion flakes
1	(4 ounce) can mushroom pieces, finely chopped	1	egg
			poppy or sesame seeds
2	tablespoons diced pimento		

Open and fold out crescent rolls into four squares. Combine cream cheese, mushrooms, pimentos, and mustard. Place teaspoon of mixture on each square. Sprinkle with dehydrated onions. Roll up squares and cut into 6 pieces. Placed on greased cookie sheet. Brush with beaten egg and sprinkle with sesame or poppy seeds. Bake at 375° for 12 to 20 minutes. Serve hot.

1904

The Jefferson Medical College was one of the first medical schools in the country to recognize the new surgical specialty of orthopedic surgery by founding a Department of Orthopedic Surgery in 1904.

Fluffy Hot Crab Dip

MAKES 1½ CUPS

½	pound crabmeat, cleaned	1	tablespoon milk
1	(8 ounce) package whipped cream cheese	2	tablespoons Old Bay Seasoning™ dash Worcestershire sauce
2	tablespoons lemon juice	½	teaspoon horseradish sprinkle of paprika
3	tablespoons mayonnaise		

Combine all ingredients (except paprika) with the whipped cream cheese; mix well using a hand mixer. Pour into a small casserole dish and bake for 30 minutes at 350°. Sprinkle with paprika. Serve hot with crackers or pita bread slices for dipping.

Marinated Shrimp

4 SERVINGS

1	pound boiled, peeled shrimp	1	tablespoon celery seed
¼	cup apple cider vinegar	1	tablespoon capers
¼	cup canola oil	1	red onion, sliced thinly
1	dash Tabasco™ sauce		

Toss cooked shrimp with vinegar, canola oil, and Tabasco™ sauce. Add celery seed and capers. Refrigerate overnight. Mix before serving. Garnish with red onions.

Soups

Mango Gazpacho, recipe page 40

1907 – The "New" Jefferson Hospital

THE NEW JEFFERSON HOSPITAL

OPENED JUNE, 1907

Tortilla Soup

A quick Sunday dinner that appeals to all.

2   cans (8 ounces) chicken broth
1   medium onion, chopped
4   ounces green chilies, diced
3   teaspoons chili powder
1-2 dashes hot sauce
2   cups skinless chicken, cooked and torn into pieces

1   cup frozen yellow corn (optional)
2   cups baked corn tortilla chips, broken into pieces
1   cup Cheddar cheese, shredded
2   small tomatoes, chopped
1   avocado, sectioned

In a medium pot, combine broth, onion, chilies and chili powder. When this boils stir in hot sauce, chicken pieces and corn. Simmer 10 minutes or until onion is tender. Ladle into bowls add corn chips and sprinkle with cheese, tomatoes and sections of avocado.

Tomato Basil Soup

3   pounds ripe plum or Italian tomatoes, cut lengthwise
¼   cup, plus 2 tablespoons olive oil
1   tablespoon salt
1   tablespoon black pepper
2   onions, chopped
4   garlic cloves, minced
2   tablespoons butter

¼   teaspoon crushed red pepper
1   (28 ounce) can plum tomatoes with juice
4   cups packed fresh basil
1   teaspoon fresh thyme leaves, chopped
1   quart chicken stock
    Parmesan cheese

Toss fresh tomatoes with ¼ cup olive oil and salt and pepper. Roast tomatoes on a baking sheet for 45 minutes. Sauté onions and garlic in remaining olive oil, butter and red pepper flakes. Add canned tomatoes, puréed, along with basil, thyme and chicken stock. Mix in oven roasted tomatoes. Bring to a boil, and then simmer for 40 minutes. Purée to desired consistency with immersion blender or food processor. Garnish with Parmesan cheese if desired.

1952

Elizabeth Bogardus, M.D. was the first woman resident appointed to Jefferson Medical College Hospital.

1876

The Centennial Exposition, the first official World's Fair in the United States, was held in Philadelphia, Pennsylvania, from May 10 to November 10, 1876, to celebrate the 100th anniversary of the signing of the Declaration of Independence in Philadelphia. It was officially known as the <u>International Exhibition of Arts, Manufactures and Products of the Soil and Mine.</u>

Soups

Jack Francis Snapper Soup

8 SERVINGS

A specialty of Jack Francis Catering in Conshohocken, Pennsylvania.

1	pound turtle meat	1	quart beef stock
⅓	cup butter	1	cup strained tomatoes
¼	cup carrots, diced	½	teaspoon salt
¼	cup onions, diced	½	teaspoon marjoram
¼	cup celery, diced	½	teaspoon pepper
2	crushed garlic cloves	1	teaspoon Worcestershire sauce
⅓	cup flour	⅓	cup dry sherry
1	teaspoon paprika		

Place turtle meat in large pot with 2 quarts of water and bring to a boil. Simmer for 2 hours. Remove meat from water and cut into ¼ inch pieces. Sauté vegetables and garlic in butter until tender. In a small bowl mix ½ cup water with paprika and flour. Stir until smooth. Add puréed tomatoes, spices and Worcestershire sauce. Stir in beef stock and bring to a boil. Simmer for 1 hour. Add meat to stock and vegetables. Bring to a boil and simmer for 15 minutes. Remove from heat and add sherry before serving.

Dark turkey meat may be used in place of turtle meat.

A Philadelphia classic!

Mango Gazpacho *(pictured)*

4 SERVINGS

Great, light, evening meal on a hot summer day — can be made 8 hours ahead.

2	mangoes, ripe, peeled and pitted	1	tablespoon fresh lime juice
1	green apple, peeled and chopped	2	teaspoons fresh ginger, peeled and chopped
1	celery rib, chopped		
¾	cup orange juice	¼	teaspoon ground cumin
¾	of a medium cucumber, peeled and chopped		cilantro sprigs (for garnish)

Purée all ingredients in blender. Chill for 2 hours. Keep refrigerated until ready to serve. Garnish with cilantro.

Minestrone

olive oil

1 red onion, peeled and finely sliced

2 carrots, peeled and finely sliced

2 ribs celery, finely chopped

3 slices of smoked bacon or pancetta, chopped

2 cloves garlic, peeled and chopped

1 leek, chopped

2 (14 ounce) cans tomatoes

3 fresh tomatoes, peeled

21 fluid ounces vegetable or chicken stock

2 white beets, washed and cut into chunks

2 potatoes, peeled and diced

3½ ounces dried spaghetti, broken into pieces

1 heart of a Savoy cabbage, shredded

few sprigs of fresh basil and parsley, leaves picked

sea salt and freshly ground black pepper

Heat a large saucepan over medium heat and add a splash of olive oil. Add onion, carrots, garlic, celery, bacon, garlic and leek, and sweat gently until soft. Add tomatoes, stock, beets and potatoes and bring to a boil. Simmer 15 minutes and add pasta and cabbage. Cook until pasta is tender and season well with salt and pepper. Chop herbs and add just before serving.

Classic Gazpacho

Easy to make and refreshing on a hot day.

2 cups red bell pepper, chopped

2 cups red, ripe tomatoes

2 cups seedless cucumbers, chopped

½ cup sweet onion (Vidalia), chopped

½ cup cilantro, chopped

½ cup parsley, chopped

2 cloves garlic, chopped

½ cup breadcrumbs

¼ cup extra virgin olive oil

2 tablespoons red wine vinegar

1½ teaspoons salt

¼ teaspoon white pepper

Blend all ingredients in a blender or food processor for 3 minutes until well blended. Chill and serve with a sprig of parsley or cilantro. Soup can be strained through a fine sieve for a thinner soup.

1844

Jefferson Medical College provided patient beds over a shop at 10th and Sansom Streets.

1897

Arthur Dorrance hires his 24-year-old nephew, Dr. John T. Dorrance. Dr. Dorrance develops a formula for condensed soups. Removal of water from soup reduces the volume of a can from 32 ounces to 10.5 ounces and the price from 35 cents to a dime.

Roasted Carrot Ginger Soup

8 SERVINGS

1½ pounds carrots, peeled and quartered lengthwise

1½ pounds parsnips, peeled and quartered lengthwise

1 large onions, sliced

1 piece (about 1½ inches) fresh ginger, peeled and chopped

3 tablespoons olive oil

3 tablespoons butter (combined with the olive oil)

3 tablespoons dark brown sugar, packed

8 cups chicken broth
   salt to taste
   pinch of cayenne pepper

¼ cup crème fraîche
   snipped fresh chives (for garnish)

Preheat oven to 350°. Combine carrots, parsnips, onion and ginger in shallow roasting pan. Drizzle with olive oil and dot with butter. Sprinkle with brown sugar. Pour 2 cups of broth into pan, cover tightly with foil and bake until vegetables are tender (about 2 hours). Transfer vegetables and broth to a large soup pot and add remaining 6 cups broth. Season to taste with salt and pepper. Bring to a boil. Reduce heat and simmer, partially covered, for 10 minutes. Purée soup in blender until smooth, adding more broth if necessary. Return soup to the pot, adjust seasonings and heat through. Garnish with crème fraîche and sprinkle with chives.

Minted Pea Soup

4 SERVINGS

This soup should be served chilled or at room temperature.

2 cups fresh or frozen peas

1 cup chopped romaine lettuce

1 cup chicken broth

½ cup finely chopped onion

½ cup 1% low fat milk

4 tablespoons chopped fresh mint

½ cup sour cream

¼ teaspoon salt

¼ teaspoon pepper

Combine first 4 ingredients in a medium saucepan and bring to a boil. Stir in milk, reduce heat and simmer uncovered for 15 minutes or until vegetables are very tender. Place mixture into a blender or food processor, letting stand for 5 minutes. Blend or process until smooth. Pour into bowls, stir in mint, sour cream, salt and pepper.

Summer Corn and Potato Soup 6-8 SERVINGS

This recipe was donated by the National Foundation for Celiac Awareness (NFCA) and is gluten free. This recipe is easily doubled.

1   tablespoon butter
    (no substitutions)

1   pound gluten free sliced bacon,
    cut into ¼ inch pieces

1   cup sweet, chopped onion
    kosher salt and fresh black
    pepper

1   tablespoon fresh garlic, minced

2   tablespoons brown rice flour
    (white rice flour may also be
    used)

4   cups fresh chicken stock
    (preferred) or gluten free
    chicken or vegetable broth

4   cups potatoes, peeled and diced

½-1 cup fresh carrot, shredded
    (optional, this gives the soup a
    nice color)

4-6 ears fresh corn (white or
    bi-color has the best flavor)

1   cup half-and-half

1   teaspoon fresh thyme
    fresh flat leaf parsley

2-3 green onions, chopped
    sharp Cheddar cheese, freshly
    grated
    cooked bacon

In a heavy stock pan, melt butter over high heat, add chopped bacon and cook until crispy. Scoop bacon out and place on a paper towel lined platter to drain and cool. Pour all fat, except 4 tablespoons out of pot. Add chopped onions and season with salt and pepper, cooking on medium heat until soft. Add garlic and continue cooking for about 1 minute. Sprinkle rice flour on onions and garlic, cook for another minute, stirring constantly. Add broth and diced potatoes. Cover stock pot and bring to a boil, then lower heat and simmer for about 15 minutes, until potatoes are tender. For a creamier soup, use an immersion mixer for about 1 minute at this time. Add corn and carrots, cover and simmer for another 10 to 15 minutes. Slowly stir in half-and-half. Add thyme, salt and pepper to taste. Sprinkle with chopped parsley and serve with garnishes.

If fresh corn is not available, use frozen white corn kernels; 8 to 16 ounces depending upon how much you want in your soup.

1839

Thomas Dent Mutter, MD, Professor of Surgery at Jefferson (1841-1856), published the first monograph on the clubfoot. His textbook, <u>Operations of Surgery</u> (1846), described amputations, injuries of muscles and tendons, contractions of the leg and thigh, ankylosis, and clubfoot.

1891

When the Jefferson Medical College Hospital first opened its doors, it did not have any nurses. Dr. Samuel D. Gross was a strong advocate for an educated nursing staff. The Jefferson School of Nursing opened in 1890 as a nurses' training program and admitted 13 students. Students received a stipend of $6.00 per month in addition to food, board and laundry service. There was no tuition.

Mediterranean Zucchini Soup
6-8 SERVINGS

Delicious hot or cold!

½	medium onion	2	teaspoons curry powder
2	cloves garlic, minced	½	teaspoon salt
2	tablespoons butter	½	cup sour cream
2	pounds zucchini, trimmed and thinly sliced	½	cup plain yogurt
3½	cups reduced sodium chicken broth		ground black pepper to taste

Sauté onion, garlic and butter in a large sauce pan until translucent. Add zucchini, toss to coat with butter. Add chicken broth, curry and salt. Cover and cook until zucchini is tender. Purée soup in a blender until smooth. If serving hot, whisk in sour cream and yogurt; add ground pepper and serve. If serving cold, chill for several hours and garnish with a dollop of sour cream and yogurt mixed.

Matzo Ball Soup with Chicken Broth
4 SERVINGS

½	cup matzo meal	¼	teaspoon white pepper
4	egg whites, beaten lightly	½	teaspoon onion powder
2	tablespoons canola oil	½	teaspoon garlic powder
2½	tablespoons water	6	cups chicken broth
½	teaspoon salt		

Combine matzo meal with egg whites, oil, water, pepper, salt, onion and garlic powders in a bowl and refrigerate for 20 minutes. Boil chicken broth. Wet hands and form matzo mixture into small balls and drop into hot soup. Cover pot and lower heat to a simmer for 15 to 20 minutes.

Curried Pumpkin Soup

6-8 SERVINGS

2 tablespoons butter	¼ teaspoon salt
¼ cup onion, finely chopped	¼ teaspoon fresh grated nutmeg
1 tablespoon all-purpose flour	freshly ground pepper, to taste
1½ teaspoons curry powder	1 cup 2% milk
2 (10 ounce) cans chicken broth	minced chives or parsley, for garnish
1 (16 ounce) can pumpkin	low fat plain yogurt, for garnish
1 teaspoon brown sugar	

Melt butter in a 3 quart saucepan over medium heat. Add onion and sauté for 5 minutes. Mix in flour and curry powder and cook until bubbling, about 2 minutes. Remove from heat and gradually stir in broth. Add pumpkin, brown sugar, salt, pepper and nutmeg. Cook over medium heat, stirring constantly until thickened. Blend in milk and cook until thoroughly warmed — do not boil! Ladle into bowls. Garnish with chives or parsley and yogurt. Serve immediately.

Barley Beef and Vegetable Soup

12 SERVINGS

1 pound beef shank	2 cups tomato juice
1 tablespoon olive oil	½ head green cabbage, finely chopped
1 large white onion, diced	1½ cups barley
8 cups vegetable broth	1 large bag mixed frozen vegetables
3 large carrots, sliced	
2 cups water	
3 stalks celery, chopped	

In a large pot, brown beef shank in olive oil. Add onion and sauté until translucent. Add water and broth along with carrots and celery. Bring to a boil. Add tomato juice. Lower temperature and simmer for 1 hour. Add chopped cabbage. Cook for 20 minutes and add barley. Cook 45 minutes, covered. Just before serving, add frozen vegetables, covering pot and turn off heat. Let sit for 5 minutes, and then serve.

1885

Philadelphia's South 9th Street Italian Market began when Antonio Palumbo, an Italian immigrant, opened a boarding house in the neighborhood for other Italians. Businesses sprang up to serve this growing community and began to form the largest, outdoor, continuous market in the country. Palumbo's continued also as a restaurant until 1994.

1877

The Jefferson Medical College Hospital was founded 53 years after the establishment of the Medical College. It was one of the first hospitals in the nation affiliated with a medical school. Located at 1020 Sansom Street, it provided beds for 125 patients.

Philly Pasta e Fagioli

6 SERVINGS

This freezes well.

1	small onion, peeled and chopped	2	tablespoons chopped Italian parsley
4	tablespoons extra virgin olive oil	1	(15 ounce) can cannellini beans, with liquid
4	cloves garlic, peeled and minced	4	cups, plus 6 ounces water
3	cups canned Italian tomatoes		salt and pepper to taste
8-10	basil leaves, snipped or ½ teaspoon dried basil	6	ounces ditalini pasta

Sauté onion in olive oil until soft. Add garlic and sauté for 1 minute. Add tomatoes, basil and parsley. Cook over medium-high heat, stirring. Add beans with their liquid and water. Cook over medium heat 15 minutes, until soup thickens. Add salt and pepper. Add pasta and cook al dente.

Spicy Crab Soup

4-6 SERVINGS

6	cups chicken stock	1	tablespoon rice vinegar
2	tomatoes, peeled and finely chopped	¾	teaspoon sugar
½	teaspoon fresh ginger, finely chopped	1	tablespoon cornstarch
		2	tablespoons water
1	small fresh red chile, seeded and finely chopped	6	ounces white crabmeat (thawed if frozen, drained if canned)
2	tablespoons Chinese rice wine or dry sherry		salt and pepper
		2	scallions, shredded, for garnish

Pour stock into large, heavy bottom saucepan and add tomatoes, ginger, chile, rice wine, vinegar and sugar. Bring to boil and reduce heat. Cover and simmer for 10 minutes. Mix cornstarch and water together in a small bowl until smooth paste forms, then stir into the soup. Simmer, stirring constantly, for 2 minutes, or until slightly thickened. Gently stir in crabmeat and heat through for 2 minutes. Season with salt and pepper and ladle into warmed soup bowls and serve garnished with scallions.

May substitute Old Bay™ for red chile.

Mother's Southern Gumbo

2½	pounds chicken pieces	1	cup water
½	cup cooking oil	1	bay leaf
1	cup diced ham	1	teaspoon crushed thyme
1	cup chopped onion	1	pinch cayenne pepper
1	cup chopped celery	1	tablespoon salt
3	cloves garlic, minced	¼	cup minced parsley
1	pound sliced okra	1	pint oysters with liquid
2	cups canned tomatoes	1	pound shrimp, shelled
1	(8 ounce) can tomato sauce		parsley and chopped scallions

Season chicken with salt and pepper. Sauté in olive oil until brown and remove from pan. Add ham and onion to pan and sauté 1 minute. Stir in celery, garlic and okra. Cook 8 to 10 minutes stirring constantly until glutinous substance from okra disappears. Add tomatoes, tomato sauce, water, seasonings, parsley and chicken. Simmer 1 hour on low heat. Remove chicken and take out bones, returning to pan once they are removed. Add oysters with liquid and simmer for 3 minutes. Add shrimp and simmer until pink. Serve in soup bowls with rice. Garnish with parsley and chopped scallions.

Salsa and Corn Soup with Chicken

3	quarts chicken broth	2	(10 ounce) packages frozen whole kernel corn
2	pounds boneless, skinless chicken breasts, cooked and chopped	4	ounces mild salsa
		4	large carrots, diced

Bring chicken broth to a boil in a 6 quart pot. Add chicken, corn, salsa and carrots. Bring to a boil. Reduce heat and simmer until carrots are tender, about 30 minutes.

1900

Activities in the early years of the Women's Auxiliary revolved around supplying food for doctors and nurses in training, providing support and care for expecting mothers, and contributing funds to cover expenses of running the hospital wards and to purchase hospital equipment.

Minnesota Wild Rice Soup

12 SERVINGS

2	cups wild rice, cooked
½	cup chopped onion
¼	cup carrots, finely grated
½	cup butter
1	cup flour
8	cups chicken broth
2	chicken breasts, baked and shredded
3	tablespoons pecans, chopped
¼	teaspoon white pepper
	sea salt, to taste
¼	cup half-and-half or milk
	curly or flat leaf parsley

Soak wild rice submerged in water for 8 hours, pour off water. Cover with fresh water; boil in a 6 to 8 quart pot until rice is fluffy. Sauté onion and carrots in butter and sprinkle with flour. Add chicken broth slowly. Transfer to a large pot. Add shredded chicken and chopped nuts. Add wild rice. Stir in half-and-half or milk. Heat gently, do not boil. Serve with a sprig of parsley.

Dash of sherry may be added when soup is served.

New England Clam Chowder

6-8 SERVINGS

6	slices bacon, diced
1	cup chopped onion
2	large potatoes, peeled and diced
8	ounce bottle clam juice
3	(6½ ounce) cans chopped clams, drained reserving liquid
2	tablespoons flour
4	tablespoons butter
2	tablespoons parsley, chopped
1	dash paprika
	salt and white pepper to taste
1	pint light cream

Cook bacon in a Dutch oven until soft. Drain off fat. Add onion and sauté until soft. Add clam juice, reserved chopped clam liquid and potatoes, simmering until potatoes are fork tender, about 10 minutes. Combine flour with enough water to make a paste and add to pot to thicken. Add thyme, butter, parsley, paprika, salt and pepper. Heat to simmer. Add chopped clams and cream. Garnish with paprika and serve.

French Onion Soup

6-8 SERVINGS

3 cups onions, sliced	1 teaspoon Worcestershire sauce
2 tablespoons butter	6-8 slices French bread, toasted
2 (10½ ounce) cans beef broth	Parmesan cheese
1½ cups water	6-8 slices mozzarella cheese

In a large covered pan, sauté onion in butter over low heat for about 20 minutes, stirring occasionally. Add beef broth, water, Worcestershire sauce. Heat to a boil and then reduce heat, simmering for 30 minutes. Serve in bowls. Topped with a slice of French bread topped with Parmesan cheese. Cover with a slice of mozzarella cheese. Brown in oven for 1 to 2 minutes to melt the cheese.

South Philly Chilled Strawberry Soup

6 SERVINGS

½ cup sugar	2 (8 ounce) containers vanilla bean yogurts
1 cup water	1 (8 ounce) container plain yogurt
2 teaspoons strained fresh squeezed lemon juice	8 ounces heavy (whipping) cream
2 pints strawberries, washed with stems sliced off (reserve 6 whole)	sprigs of fresh mint

Syrup: In a large saucepan over medium heat, simmer sugar, water, and lemon juice for 10 minutes. Place in refrigerator to cool (may require several hours). Reserve 6 perfect strawberries. Purée the rest of the strawberries in a blender, 2 cups at a time and set aside. Stir the puréed strawberries into the cooled syrup. Fold all of the yogurt and the cream into the strawberry mixture. Chill, covered, for 4 to 6 hours (or overnight). Ladle into soup bowls and garnish with sliced strawberry and mint sprig.

May be used as a dessert also.

1900

Campbell's soups win a Gold Medallion for excellence at Paris Exposition. This medallion has been featured on their labels ever since.

1895

*Joseph Campbell
Preserve Company
markets a ready-to-serve
beefsteak tomato soup.*

Mulligatawny Soup

12 SERVINGS

*Taste soup during preparation, adding lemon juice, cayenne pepper and curry as
necessary.*

1	large clove garlic
¼	teaspoon ground cumin seed
6	whole cloves, finely crushed
1	tablespoon curry powder, more to taste if necessary
¼	teaspoon ground ginger
	cayenne pepper, to taste
¼	cup butter
1	(4 to 4½ pound) roasting chicken with giblets, cut into pieces
3	celery stalks with leaves, thinly sliced
2	large onions, chopped
2	carrots, diced

1	leek, white part only, thinly sliced
11	cups defatted chicken stock
	salt and freshly ground pepper
⅔	cup long-grain rice
2	tart apples, peeled, cored and diced
1	cup plain yogurt
2	tablespoons fresh lemon juice, more to taste if necessary
1	cup plain yogurt
⅔	cup whipping cream, warmed
	fresh parsley, chopped
	lightly toasted sliced almonds, for garnish

Combine garlic and spices. Melt butter in skillet over medium-high heat. Add
chicken and sauté until lightly browned on all sides. Add giblets and sauté
until cooked through. Transfer chicken and giblets to stockpot. Drain all but
1 tablespoon fat from skillet. Add celery, onion, carrot, leeks and spice mixture
and blend well. Add a small ladle of stock and cook over low heat, stirring
constantly, until vegetables are tender. Add to chicken. Stir in remaining stock
and season with salt and pepper. Cover and simmer for 30 minutes. Remove
chicken with slotted spoon and set aside. Add rice to soup and continue
cooking for 15 minutes. When chicken is cool enough to handle, cut meat into
bite sized pieces, discarding skin and bones. Return chicken to soup and blend
in apples and yogurt. Simmer 10 minutes. Degrease soup if necessary. Stir
in lemon juice, then blend in cream. Taste and adjust seasoning. Pour into a
heated tureen and sprinkle with parsley and almonds.

Coconut-Lime Chicken Soup

4 SERVINGS

2	pounds roasted chicken, shredded	1	tablespoon soy sauce
15	ounces unsweetened coconut milk	2	teaspoons Thai seasoning powder
2	cups water	¼	teaspoon salt
¼	cup lime juice		fresh cilantro
3	medium carrots, thinly sliced		lime wedges

In a large saucepan, combine shredded chicken, coconut milk, water, lime juice, sliced carrots, soy sauce, Thai seasoning, and salt. Bring to boil, then reduce heat and simmer until carrots are slightly tender. Serve in bowls garnished with fresh cilantro and a sprinkle of Thai seasoning.

Irish Cheese Potato Soup

6-8 SERVINGS

Delicious served with warm homemade bread.

6	cups chicken broth	4	cloves garlic, minced
4	cups potatoes, cubed	½	cup margarine or butter
2	cups onions, minced	½	cup flour
2	cups carrots, chopped	4	cups milk
1	teaspoon dill weed	2	cups Velveeta™ cheese, cubes
1	teaspoon sweet fresh basil	1	teaspoon salt
1	tablespoon fresh parsley	1	teaspoon black pepper
1	cup celery, chopped		

Boil chicken broth, potatoes, onions, carrots, dill weed, sweet basil, parsley, celery and garlic for 8 to 10 minutes, until tender. In a separate pan, melt butter and add flour over a low heat. Stir until blended. Add milk and stir until thick. Add Velveeta™ cheese cubes, stir until melted. DO NOT BOIL. Add salt and pepper. Add cheese mixture to the vegetable mixture, stirring well.

1784

Mulligatawny soup is an Anglo adaptation of the Indian Tamil soup, called milagu-tannin or "pepper-water". Spicy pepper-pot soup became a favorite in England and Australia and was introduced to the American colonies, including Philadelphia, in the late 1700s.

Chilled Summer Cucumber Soup

4-6 SERVINGS

3-4 medium cucumbers	½ cup dill weed paste (Gourmet Garden™ brand is convenient)
3 tablespoons butter	¼ cup quick-cooking farina cereal
6 cups chicken stock	Salt and pepper to taste
⅓ cup onions, chopped	½ cup sour cream or crème fraîche
2 tablespoons apple cider vinegar	Fresh dill sprigs

Peel cucumbers and score. Slice one-quarter of a cucumber into ultra-thin slices and set aside. Remove seeds and roughly chop the remaining cucumbers. Melt butter in 2 quart pot and sauté onions for 2 to 3 minutes. Add cucumbers, broth, vinegar and ⅓ cup of the dill paste. Bring to a boil and whisk in farina. Simmer uncovered until farina is soft, about 20 minutes. Remove from heat and purée mixture. Reheat soup, thin with extra water or broth if too thick. Season with salt and pepper. Chill soup for several hours. Before serving whisk in the sour cream or crème fraîche. Garnish with the thin cucumber slices and fresh dill sprig.

May also be served as a hot soup.

Velvety Mushroom Soup

1 pound fresh mushrooms, quartered	3 cups milk
1 medium onion, chopped	1 cup heavy cream
1 quart chicken broth	salt
6 tablespoons butter	white pepper
6 tablespoons flour	Tabasco™ sauce
	3 tablespoons sherry

In a medium saucepan, simmer mushrooms and onions in chicken broth for 30 minutes. Blend using an immersion blender or food processor.
In a large stockpot, melt the butter, then add flour and whisk until flour is absorbed to form a roux. In a separate pan, bring milk to a boil. Add to the roux. Gently whisk until thickened. While stirring, add cream, then mushroom mixture. Add seasonings to taste. Add sherry just before serving.

Salads

Israeli Morning Salad, recipe page 62

From 1908 Jefferson Hospital Report

A Year's Work

In Wards and Rooms. . . .   3,660 patients

Emergency Service . . . .   5,689 patients

In the Dispensaries . . . .   22,153 patients

Dispensary visits, 105,950

Salad Champignon

6-8 SERVINGS

Prepare 1 to 2 hours ahead of time.

1½	pounds fresh mushrooms	¼	teaspoon salt
1	teaspoon vinegar	¼	teaspoon freshly ground pepper
	juice of 1 lemon	1	head Bibb lettuce
2	tablespoons mayonnaise	1	tomato, sliced
1	clove garlic, minced		parsley sprigs

Clean and wash mushrooms in cold water with 1 teaspoon of vinegar. Dry with cloth and slice. Sprinkle with lemon juice. Toss lightly but thoroughly with mixture of mayonnaise, garlic, salt and pepper (mixture might seem dry but will become more liquid in 1 to 2 hours). Toss lightly several times. Serve on Bibb lettuce with tomato slices and parsley sprigs.

Cabbage and Corn Slaw with Cilantro and Orange Dressing

8-10 SERVINGS

Dressing may be made up to a day ahead of time, cover and refrigerate.

⅓	cup frozen orange juice concentrate, thawed	2	medium carrots
⅓	cup rice vinegar, unseasoned	1	medium bell pepper, stemmed, cored and cut into strips
⅓	cup vegetable oil (sunflower or safflower)	6	medium green onions, sliced thin
2	(8 ounce) bags coleslaw mix	½	cup fresh cilantro, chopped
4	ears fresh corn, shucked and cut from cob		

Whisk orange juice concentrate, rice vinegar and oil in small bowl, season with salt and pepper. Combine cole slaw, corn, carrots, bell pepper, green onions and cilantro in a large bowl. Toss with enough dressing to cover and coat. Season with salt and pepper to taste. Let stand 15 minutes and toss again before serving.

The Jefferson Gray Lady Unit, a branch of the Women's Board, was the largest women's hospital volunteer unit in the U.S. and produced more than 200,000 bandages and dressings a year during World War II.

Hires Root Beer was created by Philadelphia pharmacist Charles Elmer Hires. Hires first tasted root beer, a traditional American beverage dating back to the Colonial era, while on his honeymoon in 1875. By 1876, Hires had developed his own recipe, and was marketing 25-cent packets of powder which each yielded five gallons of root beer.

Candied Almond Pear and Goat Cheese Salad with Shallot Vinaigrette

8 SERVINGS

2 tablespoons balsamic vinaigrette	2 pears, cored and cubed
1 teaspoon shallot, minced	1 cup red grapes, halved
¼ cup plus 1 tablespoon extra virgin olive oil	½ cup sweetened, dried cranberries
1½ cups slivered almonds	2 ounces goat cheese, blue cheese or Gorgonzola, crumbled
⅔ cup sugar	salt
5½ cups mesclun mix	freshly ground pepper
2 cups arugula, torn	

Place vinegar, shallot, olive oil, salt and pepper in a jar and shake until emulsified. Set aside. Cover a baking sheet with foil. In a nonstick skillet, sprayed with cooking spray, heat almonds over medium heat. Cook 2 to 3 minutes to toast the almonds, gently shaking the skillet. Slowly add sugar, cook about 8 to 9 minutes, stirring constantly with a metal spoon to keep the almonds separated as the sugar caramelizes. The sugar will turn a deep amber color. Remove from heat immediately and quickly spread the almonds onto the prepared baking sheet and separate them to prevent clumping. (Almonds may be made in advance and stored in an airtight container.) In a large bowl, toss mesclun, arugula, pears, grapes, cranberries and cheese. Sprinkle with candied almonds and coat with vinaigrette. Season with salt and pepper to taste.

Wild Rice Chicken Salad

1 cup wild rice (uncooked)

4 chicken bouillon cubes

2 green onions, sliced thin

4 cups water chestnuts, chopped

1 pound cooked chicken, cut or torn into cubes

1 cup green grapes

⅔ cup mayonnaise

½ lemon, juiced

½ teaspoon black pepper

½ cup pimento or roasted red pepper, chopped

1 cup cashews, broken

At least 2 hours before serving, cook wild rice and bouillon cubes in water until water is absorbed. Refrigerate. Add onion, water chestnuts and chicken. Mix mayonnaise, lemon juice, grapes and pimento and toss with chicken and rice. Add cashews just before serving.

May be made the day before serving.

57

1848

In 1848, Eber C. Seamen patented the first commercial ice cream machine, which made Philadelphia-style ice cream available on a national basis.

Arugula Pasta Salad

4-6 SERVINGS

½ (16-ounce) box ziti

⅓ cup white balsamic vinegar

⅓ cup olive oil
salt and pepper to taste

1 pint cherry tomatoes, halved

1 tablespoon flat leaf parsley, chopped

½ cup red onion, chopped

2 cups arugula

2 tablespoons crumbled feta

Cook ziti until al dente and set aside to cool. Combine vinegar, oil, salt and pepper. Put tomatoes, parsley, onion and arugula in a bowl and pour dressing over. Toss with pasta. Sprinkle feta on top.

A summer favorite, as a side dish or a lunch entrée.

Reading Terminal Market opened its doors. The new Market was approximately 78,000 square feet and held nearly 800 spaces for merchants, each positioned in six foot stalls.

Stacked Beet Salad

2 SERVINGS

This recipe may be doubled or tripled very nicely and presents beautifully.

2	medium beets	⅓	cup balsamic vinegar
1	teaspoon olive oil	1	teaspoon Dijon mustard
4	ounces goat cheese, room temperature	2	tablespoons honey
		1	cup olive oil
3	tablespoons toasted walnuts, chopped		salt and pepper
		2	cups spring mix greens

Preheat oven to 425°. Rinse beets and place in shallow roasting pan. Drizzle with olive oil. Cover with foil and bake until tender (about 45 minutes). Cool. Peel and slice beets thinly. Spread goat cheese on one slice, then stack beet slice on top, alternating beet slices and goat cheese until the beet is reassembled. Nestle on a bed of greens. Repeat with second beet. Mix vinegar, mustard, honey, salt and pepper (to taste) and add oil slowly to emulsify. Drizzle over beets and sprinkle with walnuts.

Beet may also be fanned to reveal the contrasting layers.

Purple Cabbage Salad

6-8 SERVINGS

½	cup slivered almonds	½	cup olive oil
2	tablespoons sesame seeds	8	tablespoons apple cider vinegar
1½	pounds red cabbage	2	teaspoons salt
8	scallions	1	teaspoon pepper
1	package ramen noodles, uncooked with 2 Oriental seasoning packets	2	tablespoons sugar
		1	teaspoon celery salt
			handful chopped fresh basil

Lightly toast almonds and sesame seeds. Chop cabbage and scallions and place in a large plastic bag with almonds, sesame seeds and ramen noodles. Put olive oil, vinegar, salt, pepper, seasoning packets, sugar, celery salt and basil in a jar and shake. Before serving, add dressing to cabbage mixture and toss. Pour in a glass serving bowl.

Middle Eastern Tabouleh

8 SERVINGS

¾ cup bulgur wheat

3 medium tomatoes, diced

1 cup onion, minced

1-2 cups parsley, chopped

⅓ cup lemon juice, or fresh squeezed juice from 2 lemons

⅓ cup olive oil

2 tablespoons fresh mint, chopped

1 teaspoon salt

½ teaspoon pepper

Soak bulgur wheat in hot water for 30 minutes. Drain well and squeeze out excess water. Mix tomatoes, onion, parsley, and mint. Add to bulgur wheat and mix well. Blend lemon juice and oil olive until emulsified. Pour over salad just before serving. Add salt and pepper.

White Bean and Asparagus Salad

6 SERVINGS

½ pound fresh asparagus, trimmed

7 sun-dried tomatoes

1 garlic clove, minced

1 tablespoon brown sugar

2 tablespoons extra virgin olive oil

2 tablespoons white wine vinegar

1 tablespoon water

1 teaspoon spicy brown mustard

¼ teaspoon salt

¼ teaspoon pepper

1 (19 ounce) can cannellini beans, rinsed

¼ cup red onion, chopped

2 teaspoons capers

1 (5 ounce) bag mixed salad greens

1 tablespoon Parmesan cheese

Arrange asparagus and sun-dried tomatoes in a steamer basket over boiling water. Cover and steam 4 minutes. Drain and plunge asparagus into ice water to retain color. Cut asparagus into 1 inch pieces. Chop sun-dried tomatoes. Whisk garlic, brown sugar, olive oil, vinegar, water, mustard, salt and pepper in a medium-sized bowl. Add asparagus and sun-dried tomatoes, beans, onion and caper, tossing to coat. Serve over salad greens. Sprinkle with Parmesan cheese.

Garnish with quartered tomatoes around edge of bowl and sprigs of fresh mint.

2008

The Jefferson School of Population Health was established in 2008, under the leadership of Founding Dean, David B. Nash, MD, MBA.

The Mike Douglas Show moved from Cleveland to Philadelphia consistently finishing among the most popular daytime television shows nearly every season. The Mike Douglas Show was the first day time television show to feature celebrities and politicians preparing unique and favorite recipes.

Splendid Raspberry Spinach Salad

16 SERVINGS

2	tablespoons raspberry vinegar	¾	cup coarsely chopped macadamia nuts
2	tablespoons raspberry jam		
⅓	cup vegetable oil	1	cup fresh raspberries
8	cups spinach, rinsed, stemmed and torn into pieces	3	kiwis, peeled and sliced

Combine vinegar and jam in blender, add oil in thin stream, blending well. Toss with spinach. ½ the nuts, ½ the raspberries and ½ the kiwis. Garnish with remaining nuts, raspberries and kiwis. Serve immediately.

Red Pear Salad

6-8 SERVINGS

DRESSING

3	tablespoons olive oil	½	teaspoon lemon juice
3	tablespoons vegetable oil	½	teaspoon honey
1	tablespoon raspberry vinegar		

SALAD

1	red pear	1	ounce goat cheese
	green leaf lettuce	⅛	cup hazelnuts, sliced

Dressing: Mix all dressing ingredients in a screw top jar and chill. Salad: In a nonstick frying pan, heat hazelnuts over medium heat to toast lightly. Cut pear in half lengthwise and core, leaving skin on. Cut into slices and place horizontally in the rim of a serving plate to form a fan shape. Toss greens with dressing and place in the middle of the pears. Crumble goat cheese and sprinkle it and the hazelnuts over lettuce and pears.

If you cannot find a red pear, just substitute another type!

Miss Joanne's Broccoli Salad
6 SERVINGS

1	head fresh broccoli, chopped	¼	cup sugar
½	cup red onion, chopped	2	tablespoons cider vinegar
1	cup golden raisins	10	strips bacon, fried crisp and broken into pieces
1	cup sunflower seeds		
1	cup mayonnaise		

Toss broccoli, onion, raisins and sunflower seeds together. Mix mayonnaise, sugar and vinegar together. Just before serving, mix bacon into broccoli mixture, add dressing and combine all ingredients using a large slotted spoon.

Spinach and Cottage Cheese Salad
MAKES ENOUGH TO FEED A CROWD!

DRESSING

1	teaspoon salt	1	cup vegetable oil
1	teaspoon dry mustard	¼	cup sugar
1	teaspoon finely chopped onion	1½	cups large curd cottage cheese
⅓	cup cider vinegar		

SALAD

2	pounds spinach leaves	½	pound bacon
1	large head of iceberg lettuce		

Dressing: Combine salt, dry mustard, onion, vinegar, and oil in blender. Blend for 1 minute. Gradually add sugar as blending.

Salad: Reserve ⅓ of dressing to add to the greens immediately before serving. Add the remaining dressing to the cottage cheese and stir. Wash and drain spinach and break off stems. Tear iceberg lettuce into pieces and combine with spinach. Fry the bacon until crisp. Crumble bacon and add to the greens. Mix greens and cottage cheese together.

May 6, 1953

Dr. John Heysham Gibbon, Jr. and his staff, at Jefferson Medical College first used a heart-lung machine, to repair a serious septal heart defect in a young woman. This was the first successful intercardiac surgery of its kind performed on a human patient.

1829

D. G. Yuengling & Son Brewing Company is established in Pottsville, Pennsylvania, under the name Eagle Brewery. The name is changed in 1873 to Yuengling Brewery. It is the oldest operating brewing company in the United States. It is the second largest American-owned brewery after the Boston Beer Company, makers of Sam Adams beer.

Salads

Israeli Morning Salad *(pictured)*

6 SERVINGS

1	ripe large tomato	5	radishes
1	cucumber	1	bunch raw broccoli
1	red pepper	3	tablespoons extra virgin olive oil
1	yellow pepper		juice from 2 lemons
1	green pepper		salt and pepper to taste
1	orange pepper	3	scallions, thinly sliced

Chop tomatoes, cucumber, peppers, radishes and broccoli into small cubes. Toss with olive oil and lemon juice and season with salt and pepper to taste. Sprinkle scallions over top of prepared salad.

Red Onion and Mandarin Orange Field Greens

6 SERVINGS

DRESSING

½	teaspoon grated lime peel	2	tablespoons honey
2	tablespoons fresh lime juice		

SALAD

1	package mixed field greens	2	ounce package unsalted cashew nuts, toasted
11	ounce can Mandarin oranges, drained	⅓	cup golden raisins
1	small red onion, sliced thinly		

Dressing: Combine dressing ingredients. Salad: Arrange field greens on a serving platter. Top greens with Mandarin oranges, onion slices, cashews and raisins. Drizzle dressing over assembled salad.

Garnish with sliced lime.

Watercress Salad

DRESSING

1   cup plain yogurt

2   garlic cloves, crushed

3   tablespoons fresh mint leaves, chopped

SALAD

2   medium zucchinis, cut into thin strips

1   handful fresh green beans, chopped in large pieces

1   red bell pepper, seeded and cut into strips

2-3 celery stalks, chopped

1   bunch of watercress (may also use arugula)

salt and pepper

Dressing: Mix dressing ingredients together in a small bowl. Season with salt and pepper. Salad: Steam zucchini and green beans until slightly crisp. Rinse under cold water and allow to cool completely. Mix zucchini and beans with the pepper strips, celery and watercress. Assemble salad on plate and spoon the dressing onto the salad. Serve immediately.

Try adding other chopped fresh herbs for different flavors.

1959

The Women's Board had 17 active committees. However, due to parking congestion in downtown Philadelphia and migration to the suburbs, participation in the Women's Board began to decline.

Aspen Kale Salad

5 SERVINGS

4   cups kale leaves
¼   cup pine nuts
¼   cup currants
1   teaspoon olive oil

splash of lemon juice
grated Parmesan cheese,
      generous amount

Chop kale leaves extra fine. Chop currants and pine nuts and then mix with kale. Add olive oil and splash of lemon. Mound ingredients in individual servings, filling a small bowl and then turning out onto plate to retain the round, mounded shape. Top with a generous amount of Parmesan cheese.

Minted Carrot Salad

6 SERVINGS

Refreshing and colorful.

1   pound fresh large carrots,
      trimmed and peeled
½   cup golden raisins
      juice of 1 large orange
      juice of 1 large lemon

¾   cup fresh mint, chopped
¼   cup fruity olive oil or vegetable
      oil
      salt and freshly ground pepper
      to taste

In a food processor or with a grater, coarsely shred carrots. In a large bowl, combine shredded carrots and other ingredients; toss to mix. Cover and refrigerate for 6 hours or overnight to blend flavors. Serve very cold.

Perfect side dish for picnics.

Cherry Tomato Salad

4 SERVINGS

| 1 | pint cherry tomatoes | 3 | ounces feta goat cheese |
| ½ | cup pine nuts | 2 | tablespoons olive oil |

Halve cherry tomatoes in a medium bowl. Toast pine nuts lightly at 350° for 5 minutes. Add to cherry tomatoes. Crumble feta cheese into the bowl. Dress with olive oil, gently mixing.

Goat Cheese, Date and Mixed Greens Salad

8 SERVINGS

Delicious as a first course salad or side dish.

VINAIGRETTE

2	tablespoons red wine vinegar	½	cup olive oil
1	tablespoon reduced-sodium soy sauce		salt
			freshly ground pepper

SALAD

| 8 | cups mixed greens, rinsed and dried | 8 | ounces soft goat cheese, cut into chunks |
| 12 | dried dates (preferably Medjool), pitted and cut lengthwise into thin strips | | |

Vinaigrette: In a small bowl, whisk together vinegar and soy sauce. Add salt and pepper to taste. Add oil in a stream, whisking until emulsified. (May make ahead and refrigerate. Bring to room temperature and re-whisk before serving.) Salad: Combine greens, dates and goat cheese in a large bowl. Toss with desired amount of vinaigrette. May also serve dressing on side.

May use fresh figs and just arugula.

Today three committees remain to carry on the work of the Women's Board; the Maternity Committee, the Martha Jefferson Department and the Pennywise Thrift Shop. Together these committees raise over $100,000 annually to support worthwhile patient-centric projects at the Hospital.

Wilted Lettuce Salad

SALAD

1	bunch leaf lettuce, torn	6	green onions with tops, thinly sliced
6	radishes, thinly sliced		

DRESSING

6	strips bacon	1	tablespoon sugar
3	tablespoons red wine vinegar	½	teaspoon pepper
1	tablespoon lemon juice		

Salad: Toss lettuce, radishes and green onion in a bowl.

Dressing: In a skillet, fry bacon until crispy. Drain bacon on paper towel. To the hot drippings, add vinegar, lemon juice, sugar and pepper. Stir well. Immediately pour mixture over lettuce and toss lightly. Crumble bacon on top of salad.

May use cider vinegar in place of red wine vinegar.

Fruity Romaine Salad

Sure to delight!

SALAD

2	heads Romaine lettuce	⅓	cup craisins
1	cup shredded mozzarella cheese	1	apple, cubed
1	cup sunflower seeds	1	pear, cubed

DRESSING

½	cup sugar	½	teaspoon salt
⅓	cup lemon juice	⅔	cup vegetable oil
2	teaspoons onion, finely chopped	1	tablespoon poppy seeds
1	teaspoon Dijon-style mustard		

Salad: Combine ingredients together in a large, festive salad bowl.

Dressing: Combine dressing ingredients adding poppy seeds last. Pour over greens mix and serve.

Arugula and Artichoke Salad

10 SERVINGS

8	cups fresh arugula	3	chopped green onions
1	(14 ounce) can artichoke hearts		reduced-fat raspberry vinaigrette
1	cup dried cranberries		
½	cup toasted pecans	½	cup feta or Brie cheese

Toss arugula, artichoke hearts, cranberries, pecans and onions together. Dress with raspberry vinaigrette and crumbled feta or slices of Brie cheese.

May use baby spinach instead of arugula.

Greek-Style Salad

10-12 SERVINGS

SALAD

	romaine lettuce, chopped in medium size chunks	10-15	Kalamata olives
3	plum tomatoes, roughly chopped	½	cup red onion, thinly sliced
1	medium cucumber, peeled and cut into chunks	4	ounces feta cheese, crumbled or sliced in small pieces

DRESSING

⅔	cup olive oil	¼	teaspoon pepper
⅓	cup red wine vinegar	1	clove garlic, crushed
1	teaspoon salt	1	teaspoon oregano

Salad: Toss lettuce, tomatoes, olives, cucumbers and olives in medium to large salad bowl. Garnish top with red onions and feta cheese.

Dressing: Mix dressing ingredients together and serve on side.

Use mixed salad greens for variety.

1792

The first record of a recipe for Philadelphia-style ice cream appeared in The Art of Cookery, according to the Present Practice by Richard Briggs.

Yukon-Red Potato Salad

May boil potatoes a day ahead and refrigerate.

1   pound small red potatoes, cut into quarters or eighths

1   pound Yukon potatoes, cut into quarters or eighths

SAUCE

⅔   cup canola oil

⅓   cup red wine vinegar

1   tablespoon Dijon mustard

2   tablespoons yellow mustard

1   teaspoon dill weed (fresh or dried)

½   teaspoon garlic salt

½   teaspoon black pepper

SALAD DRESSING

¾   cup mayonnaise

¾   cup sour cream

½   cup radishes, sliced

½   cup cucumber, chunks

½   cup celery, chopped

¾   cup green onions, chopped

5   hard-boiled eggs, chopped in chunks

½   cup red onion, thinly sliced

½   cup fresh parsley, minced

1   teaspoon Kosher salt

dash of black pepper

Place cut potatoes in a large pot, cover with water. Bring to boil, then reduce heat and cook for 18 minutes. Drain. Sprinkle with white wine vinegar and olive oil while still warm. Transfer to a large mixing bowl.

Sauce: In a small bowl, combine sauce ingredients, whisking well to mix. Pour over potatoes. Cover and refrigerate.

Dressing: In another bowl, mix together mayonnaise and sour cream. Add radishes, cucumbers, celery, green onions, and most of parsley. Gently add to chilled potato mixture. Add eggs last. Chill until ready to serve. Garnish top with thinly sliced red onions, parsley, kosher salt and black pepper.

Salad Dressings

Try these classics with any green lettuce mixtures (frisée, romaine, Bibb, curly, arugula, endive, even iceberg)!

Bleu Cheese Dressing

MAKES 2 CUPS

4	ounces Bleu cheese	2	scallions, chopped
1	cup sour cream	1½	teaspoons lemon juice
2	tablespoons mayonnaise		salt and pepper

Crumble the Bleu cheese, sour cream, mayonnaise, scallions and lemon juice. Mix well. Salt and pepper to taste.

Honey Shallot Vinaigrette

4 SERVINGS

1	small shallot, peeled	2	tablespoons fresh lemon juice
2	tablespoons balsamic vinegar	1	teaspoon powdered ginger
1½	tablespoons Dijon mustard	¾	cup extra virgin olive oil
2	tablespoons orange juice		salt and pepper
1	tablespoon honey		

In a food processor, combine shallot, vinegar, mustard, orange juice, honey, lemon juice, and ginger. Slowly add olive oil. Salt and pepper to taste.

Garnish with toasted almonds, dry cranberries, feta cheese crumbles and/or sliced pears.

1795

Victor Collet's ornamental ice creams from his Front Street shop were so popular that President Washington kept the fluted molds for them in his High Street mansion and they were judged to be equal to anything produced in Paris.

A seed money grant from The Women's Board led to the establishment of the Jefferson Chapel. Mrs. Margaret O'Donoghue was involved with the Pastoral Care Committee at Jefferson for over 40 years.

Old-Fashioned French Salad Dressing

MAKES 3 CUPS

1	can tomato soup	1	teaspoon mustard
1	cup sugar	1	teaspoon paprika
1	cup cider vinegar	1	tablespoon Worcestershire sauce
1	teaspoon pepper		

Combine all ingredients in a food processor or blender and mix well.

Refrigerates well.

Sesame-Poppy Seed Dressing

4 INDIVIDUAL SALADS

¼	cup peach or apricot white balsamic vinegar	½	teaspoon onion, minced
¼	cup vegetable oil	1	teaspoon poppy seeds
¼	cup honey	2	tablespoons sesame seeds, toasted
¼	teaspoon Worcestershire sauce		

Combine vinegar, oil, honey, Worcestershire and onion in a mini-food processor. Blend well. Stir in poppy and sesame seeds.

Can use any nicely flavored vinegar (e.g. raspberry or tarragon).

Favorite Greek Salad Dressing MAKES 1 CUP

⅔ cup olive oil

⅓ cup red wine vinegar

1 teaspoon salt

¼ teaspoon pepper

1 clove garlic, minced

1 teaspoon oregano, fresh if possible

Mix all ingredients together in a mini-food processor. Serve immediately or refrigerate.

For variety add ½ teaspoon honey and a 1 teaspoon of grainy mustard.

Country Cupboard Dressing MAKES 1 CUP

1 cup mayonnaise

¼ cup cider vinegar

½ cup confectioners' sugar

Place ingredients in a mini-food processor. Mix well. Serve on side.

Double recipe for a party salad.

Russian Salad Dressing MAKES 3 CUPS

1 cup vegetable oil

½ cup cider vinegar

½ teaspoon salt

1 teaspoon grated onion

½ cup ketchup

½ cup sugar

½ teaspoon paprika

1 clove garlic, minced

Place all ingredients in a mini-food processor. Mix well. Refrigerate before serving.

1970

Philadelphia's restaurant renaissance began with the opening by Georges Perrier of a 5-star, 35 seat, French restaurant, Le Bec-Fin.

Southwest Salad Dressing

MAKES 1½ CUPS

½ cup green chili salsa
½ cup plain fat-free Greek yogurt
1 tablespoon cilantro
1 tablespoon green onions, thinly sliced

1 tablespoon lemon juice
1 tablespoon white wine vinegar
1½ teaspoons honey
   salt and pepper

Combine all ingredients in a deep bowl. Whisk to thoroughly blend. Refrigerate or serve immediately with your favorite mixed greens salad.

Creamy Green Goddess Salad Dressing

MAKES 2 CUPS

1 cup reduced-fat mayonnaise
½ cup reduced-fat sour cream
⅓ cup green pepper, chopped
¼ cup fresh parsley, chopped
2 tablespoons lemon juice

1 garlic clove
2 scallions, including green tops
¼ teaspoon black pepper
¼ teaspoon Worcestershire sauce

Place all ingredients in a blender or food processor. Blend until thick and creamy.

Fish & Seafood

Grilled Salmon with Honey Soy Sauce, recipe page 76

VERTICAL FILE

FOURTH ANNUAL REPORT
OF THE
BOARD OF MANAGERS
OF THE
Jefferson Maternity
OF PHILADELPHIA
For the year ending November first
1896.

Brotherly Love Crab Cakes

4-6 SERVINGS

1	large onion, minced
1	ribs celery, chopped fine
2	tablespoons butter
1½	pounds crabmeat, shredded
1	tablespoon Worcestershire sauce
1	dash cayenne

	salt and pepper
½	teaspoon dry mustard
	mayonnaise
2-3	slices bread, toasted and finely crumbled
1	tablespoon butter, for garnish

Fry onion and celery slowly in butter until glossy, remove from heat. Add crabmeat. Mix Worcestershire, cayenne, salt, pepper and mustard together. Add to the crab mixture. Add enough mayonnaise to hold together. (This can be made a day ahead.) When ready to bake, sprinkle with crumbled toast. Dot with butter and place in 400° oven for 15 minutes.

Add Old Bay™ seasoning for a Chesapeake taste.

Garlic Baked Sea Scallops

6 SERVINGS

6	tablespoons clarified butter
1	pound sea scallops, rinsed and patted dry
	salt and pepper
1	clove garlic, minced

3	tablespoons chopped Italian parsley
3	tablespoons fresh breadcrumbs
	lemon wedges

Preheat oven to 400°. Place 1 tablespoon of clarified butter into 6 individual baking dishes and heat in oven until the butter begins to sizzle. Divide scallops among the dishes, leaving space around each scallop to prevent steaming. Add a pinch of salt to each dish and two grinds of pepper. Lightly sprinkle each dish with the garlic, parsley and breadcrumbs. Bake for 10 minutes and serve with a lemon wedge.

1961

Nine women are approved for admission to the Jefferson Medical College for the September class.

2011

Michael Solomonov of the Philadelphia restaurant Zahav wins the James Beard Foundation Award for best Mid-Atlantic Chef.

Oven Fried Catfish

2-3 SERVINGS

	vegetable spray
1	pound catfish fillets
½	cup milk

dry Italian seasoned breadcrumbs

olive oil

Place oven rack on highest level in 475° oven. Spray pizza pan with vegetable spray. Dip fillets in milk, then in seasoned breadcrumbs. Place fillets on pan. Drizzle olive oil over fillets. Bake about 20 minutes.

Spatula should separate fish at the thickest part.

Grilled Salmon with Honey Soy Sauce *(pictured)*

2-3 SERVINGS

2	salmon fillets (8 ounces each)	1½	tablespoons honey
½	teaspoon salt	2	tablespoons chopped scallions
¼	teaspoon black pepper	1	tablespoon finely chopped ginger
3	tablespoons soy sauce		
1½	tablespoons rice vinegar	1	teaspoon sesame seeds

Season the salmon with salt and pepper and refrigerate for 30 minutes. Mix soy sauce, rice vinegar, honey, scallions, ginger and sesame seeds in a bowl and set aside. Grill salmon over high heat, until golden brown and crust has formed (about 5 to 7 minutes). Place salmon on serving dish and pour sauce over it. Serve immediately.

Sauce can be made ahead of time.

Ben's Grilled Shrimp

4 SERVINGS

MARINADE

1	cup olive oil	3	teaspoons ketchup
¼	cup chopped fresh parsley	1	teaspoon dried oregano
3	tablespoons barbeque sauce	1	teaspoon salt
3	cloves garlic, minced or crushed	1	teaspoon pepper

SHRIMP

1	pound large shrimp, peeled, deveined and tail on	½	lemon, juiced
		1	pound fresh linguine

Marinade: Combine olive oil, parsley, barbeque sauce, garlic, ketchup, oregano, salt and pepper. Combine ¼ cup marinade and shrimp in large plastic bag. Chill in refrigerator for 2 hours. Reserve remaining marinade for pasta later. Shrimp: Preheat grill to medium heat. Skewer shrimp, discard remaining shrimp marinade. Squeeze lemon juice over shrimp. Grill shrimp for 5 minutes a side or until pink. Serve over cooked pasta. Gently heat reserved marinade and pour over pasta and shrimp. Serve immediately.

Tuna & Mango Skewers

4 SERVINGS (ALLOW 2 TO 3 SKEWERS PER PERSON).

Soak bamboo skewers in cold water for 30 minutes.

1	pound fresh tuna, cut into 1-inch cubes	1	mango, seeded, peeled and cut into 1-inch cubes

MARINADE

¼	cup orange juice	2	tablespoons grated fresh gingerroot
2	tablespoons soy sauce		
1	tablespoon olive oil	½	teaspoon dried crushed red pepper

Blend marinade ingredients. Reserve 3 tablespoons of marinade. Add tuna to marinade and refrigerate for 30 minutes. Stir once. Preheat grill or broiler. Thread skewers, alternating tuna and mango. Arrange on a rimmed baking sheet. Brush skewers with 2 tablespoons of marinade. Grill or broil for 2 minutes or until tuna has just a bit of pink remaining at center. Drizzle with reserved 2 tablespoons of marinade.

1991

The Martha Jefferson Department is one the earliest Women's Board departments. It receives requests from the Department of Psychiatry as its major project. Their fundraiser, The Jewelry Sale, was pioneered in 1991 by Mrs. Elaine Abruzzo and Mrs. Rosemary McNulty. It remains a highly successful fund raising event, having raised more than $350,000 since its inception.

1865

The Old Original Bookbinder's Restaurant is opened by Samuel Bookbinder and quickly becomes Philadelphia's most popular seafood restaurant Bookbinder's closed its doors in 2006.

Greek Shrimp with Pasta

4 SERVINGS

½	pound small rigatoni, cooked al dente	1	tablespoon fresh oregano, chopped
4	tablespoons olive oil	½	teaspoon salt
3-4	cloves garlic, pressed		dash pepper
8-10	plum tomatoes, chopped	½	cup dry white wine
¼	teaspoon dried red pepper flakes	2	pounds raw shrimp (shelled and deveined)
¼	cup fresh basil, chopped	4	ounces feta cheese, crumbled

Cook pasta, drain and put in large serving bowl. Place in oven at 200° to keep warm. In a large skillet, heat oil and add garlic; sauté for 1 minute. Add tomatoes and spices. Sauté for 2 to 3 minutes. Add wine and shrimp. Sauté until shrimp is cooked through (about 5 minutes). Add feta cheese and cook until melted and recipe is bubbling hot. Pour skillet contents over pasta and serve immediately.

Trout Almondine

2 SERVINGS

¾-1	pound brook trout fillets	2	tablespoons slivered almonds
½	cup flour	½	fresh lemon, squeezed
½	teaspoon salt	1	tablespoon fresh parsley, chopped
½	teaspoon paprika		
2	tablespoons butter, divided		

Dredge trout in flour mixed with salt and paprika. Place trout in shallow pan that has been sprayed with vegetable spray. Melt 1 tablespoon butter and drizzle over fish. Broil 4 inches from heat, about 10 minutes. Sauté slivered almonds in 1 tablespoon butter, until golden; turn off heat and add fresh lemon juice and parsley. Pour over fish.

Salmon with Cucumber Salad and Dill Sauce

7	tablespoons fat-free sour cream	4	(6 ounce) salmon fillets, about 1 inch thick
2	tablespoons plus 2 teaspoons fresh dill, divided	¼	teaspoon salt
3	tablespoons rice vinegar, divided	¼	teaspoon freshly ground black pepper
1½	tablespoons finely chopped shallots		cooking spray
¼	teaspoon grated lemon rind	¼	cup dry white wine
2	teaspoons fresh lemon juice	1	English cucumber, about 1 pound
1	garlic clove, minced		

Combine sour cream, 2 tablespoons dill, 2 tablespoons vinegar, shallots, lemon rind, lemon juice and garlic in bowl. Sprinkle salmon fillets evenly with salt and pepper. Heat large nonstick skillet over medium heat. Coat pan with cooking spray. Add fish and cook for 3 minutes. Turn fish over and cook for 1 minute. Remove from heat. Add wine, cover and let stand 3 minutes or until fish flakes evenly when tested with fork until desired degree of doneness. Using a vegetable peeler, shave cucumber lengthwise into ribbons to yield about 2 cups. Combine cucumber, remaining 1 tablespoon rice vinegar and 2 teaspoons dill in a bowl, toss gently to coat. Place about ½ cup cucumber mixture on each of 4 plates, topping mixture with a salmon fillet and 2 tablespoons sour cream mixture.

Prepare sauce up to 1 day ahead of time and refrigerate.

Blackfish, with Chef Chip Roman, (protégé of Georges Perrier and Marc Vetri), was named Best Restaurant of the Year by Philadelphia Magazine.

Scallops with Spinach, Rice and Goat Cheese

4 SERVINGS

cooking spray

1 pound large scallops

1 tablespoon olive oil

1½ cups chopped onion

2 garlic cloves, mashed

1 cup medium grain rice

¾ cup dry white wine

4 cups reduced sodium and fat chicken broth

¼ cup chopped, fresh cilantro or flat leaf parsley

1 dash saffron threads

10 ounce package frozen spinach, thawed, drained and squeezed dry

½ cup crumbled goat cheese

Heat large nonstick skillet over medium high heat. Coat pan with cooking spray. Add scallops to pan and sauté for 4 minutes or until done. Remove scallops from pan and set aside keeping warm. Heat oil in pan over medium heat. Add onion to pan and cook for 5 minutes. Add garlic and cook for 1 minute. Add rice and cook for 1 minute, stirring constantly. Stir in wine and cook for 4 minutes or until liquid is nearly absorbed, stirring constantly. Add broth, ½ cup at a time, stirring constantly until each portion of broth is absorbed before adding the next (about 25 minutes total). Stir in cilantro, saffron and spinach with the last ½ cup broth. Add scallops and cheese, stirring to combine. Serve immediately.

May substitute crabmeat or shrimp for scallops.

Roasted Halibut with Garden Vegetables

4 SERVINGS

1	medium yellow onion, diced
1	large zucchini, diced
1	large carrot, diced
4	halibut fillets
1	tablespoon olive oil, divided
2	tablespoons Japanese style breadcrumbs
	salt and pepper to taste
⅓	cup red grape tomatoes
⅓	cup canned corn kernels

Preheat oven to 425°. Combine onion, zucchini and carrot in oiled baking pan, toss to coat. Bake, covered in foil for 15 minutes, stirring occasionally or until vegetables are slightly softened. Lightly coat halibut with ½ teaspoon olive oil and sprinkle with breadcrumbs and season with salt and pepper. Add coated halibut to the softened vegetables. Bake 10 minutes. Add corn and tomatoes. Bake an additional 10 minutes uncovered or until fish flakes easily when tested with a fork. Transfer to serving platter, placing roasted vegetables around the fillets.

This also works well using cod fillets.

Paris 66 Tuna Salad

SERVES 4 FOR A LUNCHEON OR USE AS AN APPETIZER

3	cans tuna fish, preferably packed in oil (about 15-18 ounces depending on size of cans)
2-3	tablespoons prepared horseradish
2-3	tablespoons capers, drained
	juice of 1 lemon
½-1	teaspoon dried dill weed
1	small jar sun-dried tomatoes, packed in oil
¼-⅓	cup sour cream
	salt and pepper if desired
1	baguette French bread, sliced

Drain the tuna and fork-fluff it into a bowl. Add horseradish, capers, lemon juice and dill; mix well. Drain the sun-dried tomatoes and chop roughly, add to tuna mixture. Add sour cream one spoonful at a time until you reach desired consistency — the salad should hold together, but not be too creamy. Season with fresh ground pepper and salt if desired. Serve with sliced French bread, plain or toasted.

1965

Nancy Szwec Czarnecki is the first of eight women to receive her medical diploma in 1965.

2010

Jeff Michaud of Osteria wins the James Beard Foundation award for best Mid-Atlantic Chef.

Chilean Sea Bass with Mashed Potatoes

4 SERVINGS

Serve with steamed haricot verts for a beautiful presentation.

2	tablespoons olive oil	5	servings of mashed potatoes, already prepared, divided
4	Chilean sea bass fillets, 3 inches x 4 inches each	16	individual sweet potato chips, store bought
	salt and pepper to taste		

Preheat oven to 425°. Oil baking pan with olive oil. Rinse sea bass and pat dry, placing in baking pan and sprinkle with salt and pepper, turn and season other side. Bake uncovered for about 15 to 20 minutes, until opaque, but moist appearing in the center's thickest part. Spoon one serving mashed potatoes on each of four plates; top each with 3 sweet potato chips and then fish fillets. Garnish the top of each fillet with a small spoonful of potatoes with 1 chip standing from the top of each spoonful.

Soft Shell Crabs

6 SERVINGS

A family favorite!

6	medium size soft shell crabs		pinch of salt
1	clove garlic, mashed		pinch of black pepper
3	tablespoons sweet butter, softened	3½	tablespoons olive oil
3	tablespoons all-purpose flour		parsley, fresh or dried
			lemon wedges

Rinse crabs and dry well. Stir mashed garlic into butter and let stand. Dip crabs into flour, salt and pepper mixture; shake off excess. Heat olive oil with butter garlic mixture in a large, deep skillet. Add crabs and sauté each side for 5 minutes. Shake pan, cover pan and slowly cook for another 10 minutes. Sprinkle parsley over top of crabs and shake pan. Remove crabs to a warm serving plate; spoon butter drippings over all and serve with lemon wedges.

Excellent made with 3 tablespoons of Old Bay™ seasoning, as well.

Grilled Shrimp with Lemon Garlic Linguine

5-6 SERVINGS

RUB

1 tablespoon paprika
1 tablespoon garlic powder

1 teaspoon black pepper, freshly ground
2 teaspoons salt

SHRIMP

1 pound shrimp, peeled and deveined
  olive oil to coat shrimp
6-8 wooden skewers, soaked in water for 30 minutes
½ cup salted butter
1 lemon, zested finely and juiced

4 cloves garlic, minced
¼ teaspoon cayenne pepper
1 pound linguine, cooked
1 pint cherry or grape tomatoes, halved
1 cup Parmesan or Romano cheese, freshly grated

Rub: Combine paprika, garlic powder, pepper and salt in a small bowl.

Shrimp: Curl shrimp, tail tucked inside and thread onto skewers, about 4 to 5 shrimp on each one. Brush with olive oil and sprinkle the rub generously on the shrimp. Grill shrimp directly over medium high heat, turning once until evenly pink and opaque throughout, about 3 to 4 minutes per side. Melt butter in a saucepan over low heat. Stir in lemon zest and juice, garlic and cayenne. Toss half the sauce with the linguine and add tomatoes. Divide pasta into 5 to 6 servings and top each with a shrimp skewer. Drizzle remaining sauce and sprinkle cheese generously over each dish.

1969

Mrs. Gustave (Valla) Amsterdam, Chairman of the Old Market Fair raises $37,000 and organizes several successful auctions of furniture and a Plymouth automobile to benefit the Jefferson Hospital.

Szechwan Style Shrimp

SERVES 3 AS A MEAL OR USE AS AN APPETIZER

Amazingly delicious!

SHRIMP

1   pound shrimp (25-30 count), shell, cut and devein, wash, place in cold salt water, drain in colander

2-3 hot dry peppers, or ½ teaspoon crushed red pepper (warning – seeds are hot)

3   garlic cloves, minced or pressed

2   scallions (use white and green portions), cleaned and cut into ¼ inch segments

1   tablespoon fresh ginger, minced or sliced

2   tablespoons vegetable oil

SAUCE

4   tablespoons ketchup

1½ tablespoons sugar

6   tablespoons water

2   tablespoons soy sauce

½   teaspoon salt

2   tablespoons dry sherry

4   tablespoons cornstarch

OPTIONAL INGREDIENTS

1   cup cooked rice and/or 1 cup vegetables (green peas, chopped water chestnuts, Chinese mushrooms)

1   tablespoon sesame oil
    Chinese noodles

Shrimp: Prepare shrimp before hand and have ready to use. Blot shrimp dry.
Sauce: Grease another bowl and mix the sauce ingredients in it, be sure cornstarch is thoroughly mixed in. Have optional ingredients ready for the cooking phase (see next page).

COOKING INSTRUCTIONS FOR SZECHWAN SHRIMP

1. Heat a wok or deep frying pan over high heat until very hot. Add 2 tablespoons of vegetable oil. When oil is very hot, add shrimp and cook for 2 minutes. Remove shrimp from wok. Set aside.

2. Fry hot peppers until brown in wok over medium heat. Add ginger, garlic and scallions and cook 1 minute. (Add optional vegetables and cook at same time if desired.) Add sauce ingredients and stir while cooking over high heat until sauce thickens (if gets too thick, add water).

3. Return shrimp to wok with sauce. Stir until well mixed and heated thoroughly. (Add optional sesame oil if desired.) Remove from heat and serve over rice or noodles.

Pistachio Salmon

SAUCE

2	tablespoons olive oil	½	bottle sweet pink wine, (red Zinfandel or other)
3-4	shallots, finely diced	1½	cups heavy cream
3	cloves garlic, diced		

SALMON

2	tablespoons olive oil, for saucepan	2	cups pistachios, crushed salt and pepper
2½	pounds salmon fillets		

Sauce: Heat olive oil in a frying pan. Add shallots and garlic and sauté over low heat until translucent. Add ½ bottle of sweet red wine to pan and heat about 15 minutes to reduce liquid. Strain to remove garlic and onions. Add 1½ cups heavy cream to reduced wine and stir until sauce thickens.

Salmon: Rub olive oil on salmon to enable crushed pistachio to stick on one side; sprinkle with salt and pepper. Sear the nutty side in a lightly greased pan, flip once and move to a 425° oven for 10 to 15 minutes.

Serve with fresh asparagus, sautéed spinach and/or rice.

2009

The Burt-Melville Department of the Women's Board was closely aligned with the TJUH Rehabilitation Medicine Department. Although the Burt-Melville Department became inactive in 2009, The Department's Havilland Endowment Fund continues to provide funding for special projects needed by the Rehabilitation Department.

Mediterranean Red Snapper

4 SERVINGS

8 small cloves garlic

½ (6½ ounce) jar oil-packed dried
tomato halves with herbs

½ cup pitted mixed green olives

4 (5 to 6 ounce) red snapper fillets

¼ cup crumbled feta cheese
fresh oregano leaves

Peel garlic cloves and smash with a wide knife. Heat 1 tablespoon of the oil from the dried tomatoes in an extra-large skillet. Add tomatoes, olives, and garlic, cooking 2 to 3 minutes. Garlic should be a golden color. Use a slotted spoon to remove tomatoes, olives and garlic. Set aside. Save oil for frying fish. Rinse and pat dry the snapper fillets. Season with salt and pepper. Fry fish with skin side down in pan for 4 to 6 minutes, turning once. The skin should be brown and crisp and the fish should flake easily when tested with a fork. Skin may be removed before serving, if desired. Top fish with tomato-olive mixture, cheese, and fresh oregano.

May use another meaty white fish.

Marinated Grouper

4 SERVINGS

½ cup extra virgin olive oil

2 cloves garlic, minced

3 tablespoons fresh oregano,
chopped

4 grouper filets
salt and pepper to taste

1 lemon, cut into wedges

Preheat oven to 500°. Combine olive oil, garlic, oregano and grouper in a 9x13-inch baking pan. Marinate for 30 minutes, turning once. Remove from marinade. Season grouper filets with salt and pepper. Place on roasting pan and bake for about 10 minutes Fish should appear opaque and be flaky when tested with a fork. Serve with lemon wedges and mashed potatoes or orzo.

Try with halibut in place of grouper.

Seafood Casserole

1	stick (4 ounces) margarine	3	tablespoons minced fresh parsley
4	tablespoons flour	½	cup finely chopped onion
1	can evaporated milk	¼	cup chopped green pepper
¼	pound grated cheese (yellow or white Cheddar)	1	teaspoon fresh tarragon
1	drop Tabasco™ sauce	3	tablespoons cooking sherry
¼	teaspoon black pepper	3	cups shrimp, lobster and/or crabmeat, rinsed and drained
1¼	cups fresh mushrooms		
¼	teaspoon salt		

Make white sauce by melting margarine, whisk in flour and stir until flour mixture is light brown. Add evaporated milk. Stir until thickened. Add cheese to white sauce and stir until it melts. Add Tabasco™ sauce, black pepper, mushrooms, salt, parsley, onion, green pepper and tarragon to white sauce. Add sherry and seafood, mix gently. Pour mixture into a 2-quart casserole dish. Bake at 350° for 20 minutes.

Garnish with fresh herbs or toasted breadcrumbs.

1994

La Colombe Torrefaction founded by Todd Carmichael and Jean Philippe Iberti unveils its first four classic coffee blends. The company's products are organic, Fair Trade, Rainforest Alliance, Smithsonian Bird Friendly, Utz and 4C Common Code certified. The company now features cafes in New York City, Philadelphia, Chicago and Seoul, South Korea.

Fish Tacos with Slaw

Use cod or tilapia fish fillets

- ¼ small green cabbage, thinly sliced
- 1 red, orange, or yellow bell pepper, thinly sliced
- ½ small white onion, thinly sliced
- ¼ cup fresh lime juice (use 2-3 limes)
- 2 tablespoons plus 1 teaspoon olive oil
- 1 teaspoon kosher salt, divided
- ¼ teaspoon black pepper
- 3 fish fillets, de-boned
- ½ teaspoon ground chipotle chilies or chili powder
- 8 small flour tortillas taco sauce

Slaw: In a large bowl, combine sliced cabbage, peppers, onion, lime juice, 2 tablespoons of olive oil, ½ teaspoon salt and ¼ teaspoon pepper. Set aside, tossing occasionally.

Fish: Heat the remaining teaspoon of olive oil in a large non-stick skillet over medium heat. Season fish fillets with the chipotle chilies or chili powder and ½ teaspoon salt. Cook for 3 minutes per side. Break into bite-size pieces.

Tortillas: Warm the tortillas in toaster oven. Fill tortillas with fish, then slaw. Top with taco sauce.

Roasted Shrimp with Fennel, Feta and Breadcrumbs

BREADCRUMBS

4 slices any bread with crusts removed

3 tablespoons parsley
  sea salt and pepper

1 teaspoon freshly grated lemon zest

¼ cup olive oil or enough to coat breadcrumbs

ROASTED SHRIMP

1 bulb fennel, thinly sliced

3 tablespoons olive oil
  sea salt and pepper

1-2 tablespoons garlic, minced

¼ cup dry white wine (any kind that you like to drink)

1 (14 ounce) can chopped tomatoes

2 teaspoons tomato paste

2 tablespoons freshly chopped parsley (flat or curly parsley)

1¼ pounds cleaned uncooked shrimp (with tails on)

3 ounces feta cheese, chopped or crumbled (or Parmesan cheese may be used)

1 cup homemade breadcrumbs

1 lemon

Breadcrumbs: Take any bread and cut off the crust. Put remaining bread in the food processor and blend. Add 3 tablespoons of parsley, salt, pepper and lemon zest. Combine well. Add ¼ cup olive oil or enough to coat the breadcrumbs. Preheat oven to 400°. Roasted Shrimp: In a 10 to 12 inch stainless steel pan, sauté thinly sliced fennel with 3 tablespoons olive oil, salt and pepper for 10 minutes or until fennel is tender. Add garlic and sauté for a few more minutes on medium heat so garlic does not burn. Add white wine to deglaze the pan, scraping up any brown bits on the bottom of the pan from the fennel (makes sauce very yummy). Bring the sauce to a boil and cook until liquid is reduced by half. Add tomatoes, tomato paste and the 2 tablespoons of parsley. Simmer over low heat until the flavors combine, about another 10 minutes. Remove pan with the fennel sauce from heat, add shrimp to the sauce, scattering them evenly throughout the pan. Then sprinkle feta cheese evenly throughout the pan. Cover the entire pan with the breadcrumbs. Put the pan right into the oven and bake for 15 minutes. Last step is to squeeze fresh lemon juice over the pan just before serving to brighten up the dish.

Serve with fresh Italian bread and fresh arugula dressed with lemon on the side.

2010

Kevin Sbraga, chef-owner of "Sbraga" in Philadelphia, wins the Top Chef Season 7 television cooking competition.

Herbed Tilapia

1½ pounds fresh tilapia fillets
1 tablespoon olive oil
1 teaspoon dried or fresh basil
½ teaspoon dried thyme
½ teaspoon dried rosemary
½ teaspoon dried oregano
½ teaspoon dried dill weed
½ teaspoon celery seed
1 teaspoon paprika
2 tablespoons dry, fine bread crumbs
   sprig of watercress
   wedges of lemon

Preheat skillet or grill. Combine herbs and bread crumbs. Brush one side of fillets with olive oil. Sprinkle with half of herb mixture. Place herb side down in skillet or on grill. Brush other side of fillets with olive oil and sprinkle with remaining herb mixture. Cover pan and cook for 5 to 7 minutes per side, depending on thickness of fish. Turn once. (Do not turn more often, as fish will crumble.) Garnish with watercress and lemon wedge and serve immediately.

Use orange roughy or flounder in place of tilapia.

Sole Imperial

May prepare for baking 4 hours ahead and refrigerate.

4-12 ounces sole fillets
1 teaspoon margarine

IMPERIAL TOPPING

1 egg, beaten
⅛ teaspoon white pepper
⅛ teaspoon dry mustard
¼ teaspoon Dijon mustard
2 tablespoons Parmesan cheese
   lemon slices

¼ teaspoon lemon juice
¼ cup mayonnaise
8 ounces back fin crabmeat

Rinse fish and pat dry. Coat a 9x13-inch glass baking pan with margarine. Place fish in baking dish. Combine ingredients for Imperial Topping, gently folding in crabmeat as last ingredient. Top fillet with ⅓ cup Imperial Topping. Sprinkle fillets with the 2 tablespoons of Parmesan cheese. Bake at 350°, uncovered, for 15 to 20 minutes. Top of fish should be golden brown.

Elegantly scrumptious!

Meats

BEEF · PORK · LAMB

Pork Tenderloin with Basil and Prosciutto, recipe page 100

SPONSORED BY WOMEN'S COMMITTEE OF JEFFERSON HOSPITAL TO FUND OUR BOOTH "CHRISTMAS BOUTIQUE"

Designer's Gowns & Shoes by Saks 5th Ave *

Commentary by Mrs. Edward J. MacMullan

Thursday

Music by Mark Davis

October 23rd * Barclay Hotel...

Ballroom * Five O'clock

Tea and Sandwiches or a Cocktail and Sandwiches

Bring your husband — Prize for the first gentleman arriving

$5.00
per Admission

Hearty Braised Beef

This hearty dish goes wonderfully with mashed potatoes.

2-3 pound chuck roast, cubed	½ cup celery, diced
1 tablespoon olive oil	1 tablespoon parsley, chopped
1½ cups water, divided	16 ounce can tomato sauce
1 large chopped onion	1 tablespoon sugar
2 large carrots, chopped	salt and pepper to taste

Brown meat in a small amount of olive oil over medium burner. Brown quickly so as not to lose juice. Remove pieces to closely covered casserole dish. Rinse pan with water and boil. Pour over meat. Roast, covered at 325° for 1½ hours. Meanwhile, brown onions, celery and carrots. Add parsley, tomato sauce and sugar and an additional ½ cup water. Pour over cooked meat and bake for 1 more hour.

No Fail Rib Roast

Great for Sunday Dinner - this takes 3 to 4 hours to prepare and makes your whole house smell wonderful! DO NOT OPEN THE OVEN THROUGHOUT THE COOKING PROCESS!

rib roast of beef, any size	pepper
salt	

Preheat oven to 375°. Salt and pepper roast, insert meat thermometer and cook uncovered for 1 hour. Turn oven off. DO NOT OPEN OVEN!! Up to 60 to 75 minutes before serving, resume cooking by turning oven to 300°. For rare beef, cook an additional 45 minutes, for medium beef cook an additional 50 minutes, for well done, cook an additional 55 minutes. Let stand for about 15 minutes before serving. Be sure and check the meat thermometer 10 minutes before expected doneness to avoid overcooking.

1991

Among the many accomplishments for which the WB can be justly proud is a 1991 seed money grant to support a new part-time residency program in Pastoral Care. This evolved into The Department of Pastoral Care and Education.

2008

Named "The Best
Consignment Shop
on the Main line
in 2008", the
Pennywise Thrift Shop
celebrated its
50th Anniversary on
January 31, 2011.
Proceeds from the
Pennywise benefit
patient care projects
at Jefferson.

Teriyaki Beef Roast

4-6 SERVINGS

½	cup dry sherry		2	tablespoons brown sugar
¼	cup soy sauce		2	pounds beef tenderloin
2	tablespoons dry onion soup mix		2	tablespoons water

Mix all ingredients together and marinate roast overnight. When ready to cook, put ½ of the marinade in saucepan to cook down for gravy and place roast in shallow baking pan and roast at 325° until desired doneness. Slice thinly.

Meg's Marvelous Steak

4-6 SERVINGS

½	cup soy sauce		1	teaspoon ginger (dried or fresh)
¼	cup red wine vinegar		¼	teaspoon minced garlic
2	tablespoons brown sugar or honey		2	pound flank steak or London broil

Score meat. Mix first 5 ingredients and place them with steak in a strong plastic bag. Marinate for 2 hours. Grill or broil meat to desired doneness, cut on diagonal.

Pittsburgh Powder™ Beef Brisket

It's called Pittsburgh Powder, but we like it in Philly, too!

1	(3-4 pound) brisket Pittsburgh Powder™		½	cup brown sugar white onion slices
½	cup grainy mustard			

Preheat oven to 425°. Cover both sides of 3 to 4 pound brisket liberally with Pittsburgh Powder™. Place in roasting pan and bake 20 minutes, turning once. Reduce oven to 325°. Remove pan from oven and cover meat with thick layer of sliced onions. Combine equal parts grainy brown mustard and brown sugar. Pour over meat and onions. Cover pan tightly. Bake at 325° for 3 hours.

available at: www.pittsburghpowder.com

Mouth Watering Beef Tenderloin

Have your butcher trim and tie the whole tenderloin.

6	pound beef tenderloin		Pittsburgh Powder™
½	cup olive oil	3-4	garlic cloves

Bring tenderloin to room temperature. Coat the meat with olive oil. Cut deep slits in meat. Insert thinly sliced garlic cloves before applying oil and Pittsburgh Powder™ and place meat on a rack in a roasting pan. Complete the cooking process using one of the options below:

Option 1 – Preheat oven to 425°. Roast for 10 minutes. Reduce heat to 350° and roast an additional 25 minutes for rare (internal temp 125°), 35 minutes for medium (internal temp 140°). Remove from oven, cover loosely with foil, and let rest 20 minutes. Slice and serve.

Option 2 – Preheat oven to 450°. Roast 13 minutes. Reduce heat to 375° and roast an additional 16 minutes until meat reaches 125° for rare or 18 minutes until meat reaches 140° for medium. Remove from oven, cover loosely with foil, and let rest 15 to 20 minutes. Slice and serve.

Be sure to retain and use the juices!

Available at: www.pittsburghpowder.com

95

2012

The Women's Board Recognition Wall, a project initiated and developed by WB President Theresa Yeo and supported by TJUH President Thomas Lewis, was unveiled in June 2012. It honors 107 years of service by The Women's Board.

Meats

Shane's Light Chili

8 SERVINGS

1	pound ground sirloin
8	ounces hot Italian turkey sausage, casings removed
2	cups onion, chopped
8	cloves garlic, minced
1	cup green or red pepper, chopped
1	jalapeño pepper, seeded and chopped
2	tablespoons chili powder
2	tablespoons brown sugar
1	tablespoon ground cumin
3	tablespoons tomato paste
1	teaspoon dried oregano
½	teaspoon freshly ground black pepper
¼	teaspoon salt
2	bay leaves
1¼	cups merlot wine
2	(28 ounce) cans whole tomatoes, undrained and coarsely chopped
2	(15 ounce) cans kidney beans, drained
6	ounces sharp Cheddar cheese

Heat large pot over medium high heat. Add sirloin, sausage, onion, garlic, bell pepper and jalapeño. Stir to crumble to meat. Cook for about 8 minutes until the sausage and beef are browned. Add chili powder, brown sugar, cumin, tomato paste, oregano, black pepper, salt and bay leaves and cook 1 minute, stirring constantly. Stir in wine, tomatoes and kidney beans. Bring to a boil, reduce heat and simmer for 1 hour, stirring occasionally. Discard bay leaves. Serve in bowls, sprinkling each serving with cheese.

Jonne's Meatloaf

6 SERVINGS

1½	pounds ground beef
1	cup breadcrumbs
1	chopped onion
1	egg, beaten
1½	teaspoons black pepper
¼	teaspoon salt
2	(8 ounce) cans tomato sauce
½	cup water
3	tablespoons white vinegar
3	tablespoons brown sugar
2	tablespoons brown mustard
2	teaspoons Worcestershire sauce

Mix beef, breadcrumbs, onion, egg, salt, pepper and ½ can tomato sauce. Pat into loaf and place in a 9x13-inch shallow pan. Combine remaining ingredients and pour over loaf. Bake at 350° for 1 hour and 15 minutes.

Summertime Burgers

4 BURGERS

Very flavorful burger mix.

1	pound meatloaf mix (beef, pork, and veal)	½	teaspoon black pepper
1	tablespoon Worcestershire sauce	¼	teaspoon red pepper
½	teaspoon coarse salt	¼	teaspoon paprika
		¼	teaspoon garlic powder

Form four equal patties from the meatloaf mix. Sprinkle each patty with Worcestershire sauce. Mix spices together. Sprinkle each burger with the spice mixture and cook on a grill until desired doneness.

Serve on sesame buns with a thick slice of tomato, white onion and lettuce.

With American cheese or Cheddar cheese slice, this makes a great cheese burger!

Goat Meat with Fresh Herbs

4 SERVINGS

Goat meat is very popular and a staple in many countries. It is extremely lean and has only 2 grams of fat per 100 grams of meat. Goat meat has almost double the amount of iron as its beef equivalents. Enjoy this with toasted pita bread!

1	tablespoon pure olive oil	1	teaspoon white sugar
1½	pounds goat meat, cut up	3	cups water
1	large brown onion	¼	cup tomato paste
3	cloves crushed garlic	1	cup crushed tomatoes
1	teaspoon sea salt	1	tablespoon Italian parsley, chopped
1	teaspoon white pepper		
1	teaspoon ground cumin	1	tablespoon fresh thyme

Brown meat in a heavy skillet with olive oil, then set aside. Reheat pan, sauté onion with garlic, salt, pepper and cumin. Return meat to pan and add 3 cups of water. Place lid on pan and simmer for 2 hours (more water may be added if needed). Once meat has cooked, add tomato paste and crushed tomatoes. Cook for another 30 minutes. When done, stir in freshly chopped parsley and thyme.

Can be made substituting pork for goat meat.

1930

Brothers Pat and Harry Oliveri create the Philadelphia steak sandwich based on culinary influences from Abruzzi, Italy thereby improving on the steak sandwich recipe originally served in the 1700s at the Tun Tavern.

2008

The Jefferson School of Pharmacy opened in 2008, under the direction of Founding Dean, Rebecca S. Finley, PharmD, MS.

Beef Bourguignon

Your guests will think that you are Julia Child!

1	pound bacon
1½	quarts water
3	tablespoons olive oil
3	pounds beef chuck roast, cut into 1 inch cubes
	salt and pepper, to taste
2	tablespoons all-purpose flour, divided
2	large carrots, sliced
1	large onion, sliced
½	teaspoon salt
¼	teaspoon pepper
3	cups beef broth, divided (can use 2 bouillon cubes and hot water)
1	cup red wine (Pinot Noir, Beaujolais, Merlot or Cabernet)
1	cup tomato paste
2	cloves garlic, mashed
½	teaspoon thyme, chopped or crumbled
½	cup fresh parsley, chopped
1	bay leaf
1	bag frozen, small white onions
1	pound small fresh mushrooms, trimmed
3	tablespoons butter, melted
	parsley, for garnish

Cut bacon into 1½ inch long strips. Simmer bacon strips in 1½ quarts water for 10 minutes. Drain and dry bacon. Preheat oven to 450°. In a flameproof casserole dish, sauté bacon pieces in olive oil until lightly browned. Remove to a side dish, reserving olive oil in casserole.

Season beef cubes with salt and pepper. Roll cubes in 1 tablespoon flour, shake off excess. Reheat olive oil in casserole until almost smoking, add brown beef cubes and brown on all sides. Remove cubes to side dish with bacon. Brown sliced carrots and onions in same casserole dish. Pour off excess fat. Then return beef cubes and bacon to the casserole dish with the vegetables. Sprinkle with ½ tablespoon flour. Toss with ½ teaspoon salt and ¼ teaspoon pepper. Place casserole in oven for 4 minutes. Remove from oven and toss beef with remaining ½ tablespoon flour and bake another 4 minutes (beef cubes should have a light crust). Remove from oven and turn oven down to 325°. Add 2½ cups beef broth, red wine, tomato paste, garlic and herbs to casserole dish. Cover and simmer for 2 to 3 hours.

While beef mixture is cooking, sauté small onions and mushrooms in melted butter in a skillet, until butter is bubbly. Add ½ cup beef broth and salt and pepper to taste. Simmer for 20 minutes. (Recipe continues on next page.)

BEEF BOURGUIGNON CONTINUED

When beef is tender, pour contents of the casserole dish through a strainer so that juice is captured in a saucepan. Heat juice in saucepan for 1 minute. Remove excess fat with slotted spoon. Wipe out casserole dish and return contents to clean casserole dish. Pour onion and mushroom mixture over beef mixture. Pour heated juice over casserole ingredients. Garnish with fresh parsley. Serve with potatoes, noodles or rice.

May use prepared beef stew or beef cubes.

Beef Enchilada Bake 6 SERVINGS

1	pound lean ground beef or turkey	1	(10 ounce) box frozen corn, thawed
1	can reduced-sodium condensed cream of chicken soup	1	(10 ounce) can diced tomatoes & green chilies, drained
2	cups Velveeta™ cheese, cut into ½ inch pieces, divided	2	cans enchilada sauce
		6	corn tortillas, cut in half

Preheat oven to 350°. Brown ground meat or turkey in a large skillet, drain well. Stir in chicken soup, 1 cup of Velveeta™ cheese, corn and diced tomatoes with green chilies. Cover the bottom of an 8-inch square baking dish with a layer of enchilada sauce. Spoon ⅓ of meat mixture over sauce. Cover with 6 tortilla halves. Repeat layer of sauce, meat mixture and tortillas. Top tortillas with remaining meat sauce. Sprinkle remaining Velveeta™ on top. Cover with aluminum foil. Bake for 25 minutes or until bubbly and heated through.

May add 16 ounces pinto beans, if desired. Try ground turkey for a change of pace. May use flour tortillas in place of hard tortillas.

1982

Leah M. Lowenstein becomes first woman Dean of JMC and first woman dean of any U.S. coeducational medical school.

Old Fashioned Beef Stroganoff
6 SERVINGS

4	tablespoons flour	1	cup mushrooms
1	pound beef sirloin, cut into ¼ inch wide strips and about 2 inches long		salt and pepper, to taste
2	tablespoons butter	1	can beef broth
½	cup chopped onion	1	cup sour cream
			fresh chopped chives

Place flour in a plastic ziplock bag and add meat cubes. Shake to coat with flour. Sauté meat in butter. Add onions and mushrooms. Season with salt and pepper. Cook for 5 minutes. Add beef broth and broil to thicken sauce. Mix in sour cream just before serving.

Best when served over homemade egg noodles.

Pork Tenderloin with Basil and Prosciutto *(pictured)*
4 SERVINGS

1¼	pound pork tenderloin	2	tablespoons sun-dried tomato paste or sun-dried tomato spread
	pinch of salt and pepper		
	fresh basil leaves		
2	tablespoons grated Parmesan cheese	6	slices prosciutto, sliced thinly
		2	teaspoons olive oil

Trim fat from tenderloin. Slice a pocket into tenderloin and open it flat. Season with salt and pepper. Lay basil leaves across the hinge. Mix grated cheese and sun-dried tomato paste and spread on top of basil. Fold meat to close. On waxed paper place prosciutto side by side, overlapping slightly. Place tenderloin along bottom edge of slices and roll up to wrap prosciutto around the pork. Secure with toothpicks. Brush meat with olive oil. Roast, seam side down, on rack in roasting pan for 35 to 40 minutes. Allow to stand for 10 minutes, remove toothpicks and slice.

Goulash

This may be prepared ahead and freezes well.

3	tablespoons vegetable oil, divided
2	pounds chuck roast cut into 1 inch pieces
1	onion, finely chopped
2	ribs celery, finely chopped
1	clove garlic, minced
3	tablespoons all-purpose flour
2	(14 ounce) cans chicken broth
10	ounces mushrooms, chopped

3	tablespoons Hungarian paprika
3	tablespoons tomato paste
1	red pepper (sweet), seeded and chopped
½	cup sour cream
	salt
	pepper
	egg noodles, cooked immediately prior to serving

Heat 1 tablespoon of oil in large pot. Sear the beef in batches over high heat until brown. Salt and pepper to taste. Transfer beef to plate. Heat remaining 2 tablespoons of oil, add onions and celery and cook until soft. Add garlic and cook for 1 minute. Add flour and toss to combine. Pour chicken broth while stirring constantly until thickened and bubbling. Add mushrooms, paprika, tomato paste and browned meat with accumulated juices. Simmer for 1½ to 2 hours. Add red pepper and cook 30 minutes longer. Remove from heat. Whisk sour cream with ½ cup of cooking liquid, then stir into the goulash. Serve over buttered noodles.

Pork Medallions

2-3	tablespoons butter
3-4	pork medallions
2	small onions, chopped
1	apple, sliced
⅓	cup chili sauce

1	teaspoon salt
	pinch thyme
⅓	teaspoon pepper
1	orange, sliced

Heat butter in large skillet. Brown then sear pork. Remove and keep warm. Sauté onions. Add all other ingredients, mixing well, adding orange last. Return pork to skillet. Cover and simmer slowly for 1 hour.

1968

Martha Southard is first woman to become a Full Professor at Jefferson.

2006

DiBruno's Market is recognized as the Gourmet Retailer of the Year by the National Association for the Specialty Food Trade.

Sausage and Spinach Pie

6-8 SERVINGS

Freezes well.

1	pound sweet Italian sausage, removed from casing and chopped	⅔	cup ricotta cheese
6	eggs	½	teaspoon salt
2	(10 ounce) packages frozen spinach, thawed and water squeezed out	⅛	teaspoon pepper
1	(16 ounce) package mozzarella cheese, shredded	⅛	teaspoon garlic powder
			prepared pie pastry for a 10 inch, 2 crust pie

In a 10 inch skillet, cook sausage until well browned over medium heat (about 10 minutes) stirring frequently. Spoon off fat. Reserve 1 egg yolk. In large bowl, combine remaining eggs with sausage, spinach, mozzarella cheese, ricotta cheese, salt, pepper and garlic powder; set aside. Divide pie pastry into 2 pieces, one slightly larger and roll 2 inches larger than a 10 inch pie plate. Line pie plate. Fill with ingredients. Roll remaining pie crust for top of pie, cutting a small circle in the center. Place over filling and cut slits in top. In a small bowl combine remaining egg yolk with water and brush over top of pie. Bake in 375° oven for 1 hour, 15 minutes. Let stand for 10 minutes.

Root Beer Pulled Pork Barbecue

10 SERVINGS

6	pounds pork shoulder	1	(12 ounce) can root beer
	salt and pepper	1	(18 ounce) bottle barbecue sauce
	garlic salt	1	onion, chopped

Trim excess fat from pork. Rub with salt, pepper and garlic salt to taste. Place in crockpot sprayed with cooling oil. Poke holes in pork. Pour root beer over pork. Place chopped onions in crockpot and cook on low for 6 to 7 hours until pork will shred easily. Remove pork from crockpot; discard liquid, shred pork and return to crockpot. Stir in barbecue sauce. Heat on low for 1 more hour.

Thyme Sautéed Pork Chops with Apple Slices

½ cup all-purpose flour
   Kosher salt and black pepper
8 pork loin chops
   (about ½ inch thick)
2 tablespoons unsalted butter
2 tablespoons extra virgin olive oil

16 sprigs fresh thyme
    (2 tablespoons dried thyme
    may be substituted)
2   Granny Smith or McIntosh
    apples, unpeeled and cut into
    ¼ inch slices
½-1 cup apple cider

Season the flour with salt, pepper and 1 tablespoon dried thyme or 8 sprigs fresh thyme. Pat pork chops dry and dredge lightly in flour. Heat half the butter and oil in a large skillet. Sauté half the chops for 5 minutes on each side. While chops are cooking, put some thyme under each so the herb will stick to the meat. Sprinkle more on top of chops. Remove the chops and keep warm. Add remaining oil and butter to skillet and cook the rest of the chops in the same way. Remove and keep warm. Using same skillet, sauté apples for 2 to 4 minutes adding cider to help deglaze the pan, until soft (but not mushy). Serve with apples on top.

Marinated Pork Loin Roast

12 SERVINGS

¼ cup soy sauce
¼ cup bourbon
2 tablespoons brown sugar
5 pounds pork loin roast
½ cup sour cream

½   cup mayonnaise
1   tablespoon dry mustard
1½ teaspoons balsamic vinegar
2-3 dried scallions, chopped

Mix soy sauce, bourbon and brown sugar to make marinade. Marinate pork tenderloin overnight. Drain and reserve marinade. Roast in a 325° oven for 1½ hours, basting with marinade every 15 minutes. While pork is roasting, mix sour cream, mayonnaise, dry mustard, balsamic vinegar and scallions together to make a sauce. Slice pork tenderloin and serve with sauce.

2007

Philadelphia restaurateur José Garcés, wins the 2009 Iron Chef competition. He successfully defended his title in 2010.

Shredded Pork with Noodles and Cabbage

4 SERVINGS

4	ounces bean thread noodles
12	ounces boneless pork chops
1	teaspoon cornstarch
3	tablespoons soy sauce
1	teaspoon Chinese rice cooking wine (dry sherry may be substituted)
1	spring onion (may substitute white and light green parts of 2 scallions)
¼-½	Napa cabbage (8 to 10 ounces, total)
3	tablespoons canola oil
¼	inch slice unpeeled gingerroot
½	cup chicken broth

Place bean thread noodles in a large bowl and cover with hot tap water. Soak for 10 minutes to soften, then drain carefully to keep the strands together as much as possible. Cut the noodles into 6 inch lengths. Meanwhile trim the fat from pork then cut chops in half horizontally. Stack the halves, cut meat into ⅛ inch shreds. Place in bowl and add cornstarch, soy sauce and rice wine. Stir to mix well and coat evenly. Cut the white and most of the green parts of the onion crosswise to thick slices. Cut the cabbage into 1½ to 2 inch chunks to yield 6 to 7 cups. Heat oil in wok or large cast iron skillet over high heat. Add ginger, when it sizzles, add onion and stir-fry for about 15 seconds. Stir in pork mixture, stir-fry for about 1 minute. Add cabbage in 2 to 3 additions and stir-fry for 2 to 3 minutes. Add broth and stir to dislodge any browned bits. Reduce heat to medium and cover. Cook for 4 minutes. Uncover, add noodles and stir to combine. Cook for 2 minutes until noodles are glassy and pork is cooked through. Discard ginger and serve immediately.

South Broad Street Pulled Pork

4	pork tenderloin fillets (there are two in package) – if frozen, defrost first	2	medium onions, sliced fine
1	cup water		spritz of balsamic vinegar
½	cup vegetable oil, divided		hot pepper flakes
	salt and pepper		Kaiser rolls
			shredded sharp provolone

Have slow cooker ready to use. In a frying pan, place thinly sliced onion with few tablespoons of sizzling hot oil. Cook onion until brown/caramelized. Place pork into the slow cooker. Add oil, water; sprinkle with a bit of salt and pepper and red hot pepper flakes. Add caramelized onions and spritz of vinegar. Turn slow cooker to LOW for 4 to 6 hours. Check on meat every hour or so, and if the fluid dries up, add another half cup of water. After 4 to 6 hours, the fluid should be rich and flavorful and the pork as tender as butter. Use two forks to shred the pork tenderloins. Serve on fresh bakery Kaiser roll. Sprinkle shredded sharp provolone cheese onto sandwich. Splash some of the natural juice onto the sandwich before serving.

May use a red barbecue sauce on sandwich.

Some folks like it with wilted spinach, sautéed in olive oil and garlic.

2009

Jennifer Carroll, a Philadelphia native, and Chef de Cuisine of 10 Arts by Eric Ripert, was a finalist in the Top Chef television cooking competition.

1967-1969

John Y. Templeton, III, MD, was a modern pioneer of cardiothoracic surgery. He trained under Dr. Gibbon and helped to develop the first heart-lung machine in the United States.

Lamb Kebabs with Tzatziki Sauce

4 KEBABS

SAUCE

2	(8 ounce) containers plain yogurt
2	cucumbers, peeled, seeded and chopped finely
1½	tablespoons olive oil
1	tablespoon fresh dill, chopped
2	cloves garlic, peeled
	juice of 1 small lemon
	salt and pepper to taste

KEBABS

⅓	cup olive oil
1	pound lamb, cut in cubes
⅓	teaspoon paprika
⅓	teaspoon allspice
½	teaspoon cumin
1	small onion, grated
1	garlic clove, minced
	juice of 1 lemon
	fresh rosemary and lemon thyme sprigs

Sauce: In a food processor or blender, combine all sauce ingredients and mix until well blended. Store in a covered container and refrigerate for 1 hour before using.

Kebabs: Mix olive oil, paprika, allspice, cumin, onion, garlic and lemon juice together in a bowl. Place lamb cubes in a 9x13-inch baking pan and pour mixture over kebabs to coat. Cover and refrigerate for 6 to 8 hours. Rotate kebabs once to evenly marinate. Place 4 or 5 cubes of meat on a skewer. Grill on a wood, charcoal or propane grill until desired doneness pasting with Tzatziki sauce. May serve unused sauce on side with kebabs.

May use beef, pork or chicken meat for kebabs.

Roasted Rack of Lamb

6-8 SERVINGS

MARINADE

½	cup dry red wine
½	cup orange juice
½	cup soy sauce
3	large garlic cloves, crushed and chopped

¼	cup fresh mint leaves, chopped
1½	tablespoons gingerroot, minced
1½	tablespoons wasabi powder

MEAT

3	French-cut racks of lamb (6 chops per rack), trim well
9	tablespoons seasoned breadcrumbs

1½	tablespoons melted butter
	fresh rosemary, for garnish

Marinade: Mix marinade ingredients, except wasabi powder, together in a medium bowl. Mix wasabi powder with ¼ of the prepared marinade. Stir remainder of wasabi powder into the marinade.

Meat: Place lamb racks in a large ziplock bag and pour the marinade over lamb. May divide lamb and use 2 bags. Seal tightly and refrigerate for 8 hours or overnight. Turn the bag(s) several times.

Preheat oven to 500°. Place a metal rack inside a roasting pan and spray with cooking oil. Remove lamb racks from bags and pour marinade into a microwaveable bowl; heat for 1 minute. Place lamb with top side up on the roasting rack. Roast for 20 minutes, basting several times. Remove lamb from oven. Reduce heat to 350°. Sprinkle 3 tablespoons of breadcrumbs on top of each rack. Drizzle breadcrumbs with melted butter and then 1 tablespoon of the remaining marinade. Return lamb to oven for another 15 to 20 minutes. A meat thermometer should read 135° for medium-rare meat. Remove from oven, tent with aluminum to preserve heat while meat rests for 5 minutes. Carve chops between the bones. Serve with oven roasted potatoes and baby carrots. Garnish plate with fresh rosemary.

Veal Oscar

2 SERVINGS

This recipe was donated by The Prime Rib in Philadelphia.

ARTICHOKE PURÉE

2	large artichokes, leaf and choke removed	¼	cup mascarpone
1	cup milk	¼	cup goat cheese
1	cup heavy cream	1	pinch salt and black pepper
		1	teaspoon sweet butter

CHORON SAUCE

1	medium shallot	¼	pound clarified sweet butter
¼	fresh ground pepper	1	teaspoon tarragon, minced
¼	cup white wine	2	egg yolks
2	teaspoons water	1	teaspoon tomato paste
½	teaspoon salt		

VEAL

6	medallions of veal	8	ounces artichoke purée
2	(8 ounce) lobster tails	6	ounces Choron Sauce
1	pinch salt and black pepper	2	sprigs tarragon
10	asparagus spears		

Artichoke Purée: Purée ingredients and set aside.

Choron Sauce: Combine shallots, pepper, wine, water and salt over high heat. Reduce to 2 tablespoons of liquid. Strain and cool. Whisk egg yolks in a bowl over simmering water. Add 2 tablespoons cold butter. Whisk until butter melts. Add the shallot mixture. Melt remaining butter in a saucepan. Drop by drop, add melted butter to egg yolk mixture. Whisk constantly. Add tomato past last. Set aside.

Veal: Season veal and lobster with salt and pepper and sauté in pan until cooked medium. Sauté asparagus for 3 to 5 minutes until cooked. Place a 2 ounce scoop of Artichoke Purée in center of the plate. Place the veal and lobster so that they cover the purée. Place asparagus on top, and drizzle 2 ounces of Choron Sauce on the asparagus and veal and around the plate. Garnish with tarragon sprig.

Veal Deluxe

4-5 SERVINGS

2	pounds lean stewing veal	4	tablespoons vegetable oil
1	teaspoon paprika	1	clove garlic, finely crushed
1	teaspoon salt	½	cup onion, minced
⅛	teaspoon fresh rosemary, minced	1	cup chicken broth
3	tablespoons flour	½	cup dry white wine
		¼	cup sour cream

Trim fat from meat and cut into medium chunks. Combine paprika, salt, rosemary and flour and dredge meat. Heat oil in heavy skillet and brown meat on all sides over medium high heat. Add garlic, onion, broth and wine. Cover tightly and simmer until meat is tender, about 1½ hours. Immediately before serving, stir in sour cream. Excellent served with noodles.

Easy Veal Stew

6 SERVINGS

This recipe is great served over spaetzle, noodles or rice and can be prepared ahead of time because it freezes well.

3	tablespoons olive oil	4	tablespoons balsamic vinegar
3	pounds veal cubes	1	(14½ ounce) can diced tomatoes
1	cup chopped onion	1	teaspoon dried rosemary
1	(14½ ounce) can beef broth		salt and pepper to taste

Heat oil in a 4 to 6 quart stock pot. Brown veal, a few cubes at a time, then remove from pot. Sauté onions in the stockpot. Mix broth, vinegar, tomato and rosemary and add to pot. Return meat to pot. Mix well. Cover and simmer over low heat for about 1 hour or until meat is tender. Season with salt and pepper.

1917

A Philadelphia company, Goldenberg's® Peanut Chews® candies were developed in 1917 by the Goldenberg family and used by the U.S. military during World War I

Moussaka

BÉCHAMEL SAUCE

4	large eggs
¼	cup butter
¼	cup flour
2	cups milk

½	teaspoon salt
	dash of pepper
½	cup Parmesan cheese, grated

MOUSSAKA

7	medium potatoes, peeled and sliced ⅛ inch thick
1	tablespoon olive oil
1	large onion, chopped
1	clove garlic, minced
1½	pounds ground beef
1	(16 ounce) can tomato sauce and 1 can water
½	cup red wine

¼	cup parsley, chopped
1	teaspoon dried mint, crushed
1	teaspoon cinnamon
1	teaspoon salt
¼	teaspoon pepper
1	teaspoon allspice
2	tablespoons lemon juice
1	tablespoon butter

Sauce: Beat eggs until frothy. Melt butter in a heavy saucepan. Stir in flour until it is absorbed. Remove from heat. Gradually stir in milk. Cook over medium heat, stirring constantly until mixture thickens and comes to a boil. Remove from heat. Stir a small amount of the sauce into the beaten eggs. Then gradually pour egg mixture into saucepan. Blend in salt, pepper and Parmesan cheese.

Moussaka: Peel and slice potatoes and place in a bowl of cold water. Heat oil in skillet. Sauté onion and garlic. Add meat. Brown until no longer pink. Drain. Add tomato sauce, water, wine, spices salt and pepper to meat mixture. Simmer, uncovered for 5 minutes. Butter a 3 quart oblong baking dish. Drain potato slices. Arrange slices on bottom of baking pan. Sprinkle lightly with salt and pepper. Pour half of sauce of over potatoes. Spread meat mixture over sauce. Pour remaining sauce over all. Bake at 375° for 1 hour or until potatoes are tender and top is brown.

Prepare using ground lamb or turkey for a change of pace.

Poultry

Roasted Chicken with Vegetables, recipe page 113

Womens' Board President 1921-1942
Mrs. J. Dobson Altemus
(served as President of the Women's Board for 21 years)

Roasted Chicken with Vegetables *(pictured)*

6 SERVINGS

4	garlic cloves		1	orange, quartered
1	tablespoon chopped fresh rosemary		1	pound red potatoes, quartered
1	tablespoon chopped fresh thyme		2	red onions, cut into 5 wedges each
1	tablespoon chopped fresh tarragon		3	plum tomatoes, quartered lengthwise
1	tablespoon olive oil		1	pound whole mushrooms, quartered
¾	teaspoon salt			
1	(3½ pound) chicken			

Preheat oven to 425°. Spray an 11x16-inch roasting pan with cooking spray. Chop 1 clove of garlic. Combine garlic, rosemary, thyme, tarragon, oil and ¼ tablespoon of salt in small bowl to make a paste. Gently loosen skin from the breast and leg portions of the chicken and run paste evenly under the skin. Place the orange in the cavity of the chicken. Place chicken, breast side up, in the pan. Combine the remaining 3 garlic cloves, potatoes, onions, tomatoes, mushrooms and the remaining ½ teaspoon salt in a large bowl. Spray with non stick spray and toss until coated. Arrange vegetables around the chicken. Roast, stirring vegetables occasionally for 45 to 60 minutes until inside temperature of the chicken reaches 180° and the vegetables are tender.

2000

The Scott Memorial Library of Thomas Jefferson University is home to the Solis-Cohen Family collection (1838-1960). At 110 linear feet, the Solis-Cohen family papers are the largest collection of manuscript materials held by Thomas Jefferson University Archives and Special Collections Department. Dating from the early 1850s through 1960, the collection documents one of the most significant eras in the history of medicine through the papers of one of the most prominent Jewish families in the Philadelphia area.

Poultry

1947

Frankford Candy & Chocolate Company was founded by Sam Himmelstein. It is one of the largest producers of chocolate rabbits in the U. S., making over 100 varieties.

Liberty Bell Chicken

6 SERVINGS

6	chicken skinless boneless breasts	3	tablespoons butter
1	red bell pepper, chopped	½	cup pesto sauce
1	small onion, chopped	¼	cup chicken broth
1	clove garlic, chopped	¼	cup mayonnaise
½	cup fresh mushrooms, chopped	¼	cup Dijon mustard
½	cup pine nuts, divided	¼	cup Parmesan cheese
	Crazy Jane's Seasoning™		

Pound chicken as thin as possible (in order to facilitate rolling) and score lightly on one side. Sauté bell pepper, onion, garlic, mushrooms, ¼ cup of pine nuts and crazy salt in butter. Spread pesto over the unscored side of chicken, then spoon sautéed mixture over the chicken (do not spread too thickly). Roll chicken, enclosing the mixture and secure with toothpicks. Place in baking dish, cover with chicken broth. Spoon remaining mixture over chicken. Bake for 30 minutes at 350°. Combine mayonnaise, mustard and cheese in a bowl. Place spoonful of mayonnaise mixture on plate and top with chicken breasts. Sprinkle with remaining pine nuts. Remove toothpicks before serving.

Use chopped cashews instead of pine nuts. Spinach soufflé may be substituted for pesto.

Chicken Puttanesca

2-4 SERVINGS

1	tablespoon olive oil	1	teaspoon capers
2-3	cloves garlic	5-6	Kalamata olives
1	teaspoon anchovy paste (optional)	1½-2	cups cooked chicken, cut into chunks
1	(15 ounce) can diced tomatoes	¼	pound gemelli pasta, cooked
1	(8 ounce) can tomato sauce		

Sauté garlic in olive oil with anchovy paste for about 1 minute in frying pan. Add diced tomatoes, tomato sauce, chicken, capers and olives. Salt to taste. Simmer 10 to 20 minutes. Toss with cooked pasta.

Slow Cooker Italian Chicken and Vegetables

1½	pounds boneless, skinless chicken breasts		1	(8 ounce) package low fat cream cheese
3	cups broccoli florets		1	can 98% fat free, condensed cream of chicken soup
3	cups whole mushrooms		3	cups brown rice, cooked
1	package dry Italian dressing mix			
¼	cup water			

Spray liner of crockpot with nonstick spray. Place chicken, broccoli and mushrooms in the crockpot. Mix Italian dressing mix and water. Pour over chicken and vegetables. Cover and cook on high for 4 hours or low for 8 hours. Mix together cream cheese and soup in a separate bowl. Carefully remove chicken from the crockpot to a plate. Pour cream cheese/soup mixture into crockpot and mix together with dressing and vegetables in the crockpot. Return chicken to crockpot and mix gently to shred chicken. Turn crockpot to low until heated through. Serve over brown rice.

To thin the sauce, add skim milk in very small quantities.

Chicken Scampi

6 SERVINGS

3-4	boneless chicken breasts		2	tablespoons white wine
2	eggs, beaten		1	tablespoon white wine vinegar
½	pound butter			Italian seasoned breadcrumbs
2	teaspoons parsley flakes		¼	cup Parmesan cheese
2	cloves garlic, pressed			

Cut chicken into 1 inch strips and dip in egg and breadcrumbs. Place in 9x13-inch baking dish. Melt butter, parsley, garlic, wine, vinegar and Parmesan cheese on stove and heat for about 5 minutes. Baste chicken with ½ of the sauce mixture. Bake at 400°. Every 10 minutes, re-baste chicken with butter mixture for a total cooking time of 30 minutes. Be careful not to overbake.

Do not overbake!

Chicken Poppy

2-3 pounds boneless chicken breasts

8 ounces light non-fat sour cream

1 can reduced-sodium cream of chicken soup

1½ tablespoons wine vinegar

1 sleeve butter crackers

1 stick butter, melted (or margarine)

1 tablespoon poppy seeds

Cook chicken on baking sheet in oven for 20 minutes at 350°. Cut into chunks and place on the bottom of a 9x13-inch pan. In a large bowl, mix sour cream and soup, add wine vinegar to thin. Pour mixture on top of chicken. In a small bowl, crush crackers and mix with melted butter and poppy seeds. Sprinkle evenly on top of chicken mixture. Bake at 325° for 30 minutes.

Chicken Marsala with Mushrooms and Artichokes

6 boneless chicken breasts, pounded thin

salt

pepper

3 tablespoons butter

6 cloves garlic, crushed

¼ pound mushrooms, sliced

1 can artichoke hearts, drained and quartered

3 tablespoons dry Marsala wine

1 tablespoon lemon juice

Season chicken breasts with salt and pepper. Melt butter over medium heat in pan. Add half the crushed garlic and sauté for 1 minute. Add chicken and cook until lightly browned, about 3 minutes per side. Remove to a plate. Add oil to pan and sauté remaining garlic. Add mushrooms and sauté until tender. Add artichokes and cook until heated through. Add wine and lemon juice. Bring to a boil and stir until mixture thickens. Pour over chicken. Serve with rice or pasta.

Chicken Cacciatore

4 SERVINGS

1	cup all-purpose flour	4	red bell peppers, cut into strips
2	chicken boned breasts	1	onion, sliced thin
2	whole chicken legs	2	ripe tomatoes, chopped
1	egg	½	lemon, sliced
1	cup milk	1	tablespoon capers
½	cup olive oil	1	cup dry white wine
2	garlic cloves		

Put flour in bag, add chicken and shake. Whisk egg and milk together, coating chicken. Dredge chicken in flour again. Heat oil in large frying pan. Add chicken and brown on all sides. Add garlic, red peppers, onion, tomatoes, lemon, capers and wine. Cover and cook for 45 minutes on medium heat or until chicken is cooked through.

Chicken and Broccoli Braid

8-10 SERVINGS

2	cups cooked chicken, chopped	½	cup mayonnaise
1	cup broccoli, chopped	1	teaspoon dried dill
1	cup red bell pepper, chopped	2	(8 ounce) packages seamless dough sheets
4	ounces shredded Cheddar cheese	1	egg white, lightly beaten

Preheat oven to 375°. In a large bowl, mix chicken, broccoli, red pepper, cheese, mayonnaise and dill. Unroll 1 package of dough. Arrange longest sides of dough across a 9x13-inch baking sheet. Repeat with remaining package of dough. Seal dough where they meet in the middle. On longest sides, cut dough into strips, 1½ inches apart, 3 inches deep (there should be 6 inches in the center for the filling). Spread chicken mixture evenly over the middle of the dough. To braid, lift strips of dough across mixture to meet in center, twisting each strip one turn. Continue alternating strips to form a braid. Tuck ends up to seal at end of the braid. Brush egg white over dough. Bake 25 minutes or until golden brown. Cut and serve warm.

1893

The first peanut butter grinder was patented by A. W. Straub & Co. in PA.

2010

Philadelphia Chef Marc Vetri defeats Michael Symon on the Iron Chef television show.

Soy Chicken Legs

4 SERVINGS

3	pounds chicken legs	¼	cup soy sauce
3	tablespoons olive oil	⅓	cup brown sugar
2	tablespoons fresh ginger, chopped	¼	cup rice wine vinegar
2	tablespoons fresh garlic, chopped	½	teaspoon black pepper
		4	scallions, cut 3 inches long

Wash and dry chicken legs. In a large pan, heat olive oil and stir-fry the chopped ginger and garlic until fragrant. Add chicken legs and sauté over medium heat until brown. Slowly add soy sauce, brown sugar and rice vinegar. Cover and cook 30 minutes over medium heat, or until chicken is cooked through. Mix scallions and black pepper with chicken and cook over high heat for 2 minutes and remove to serving plate.

Indian Curry

4-5 SERVINGS

3	apples, diced	1	tablespoon cider vinegar
1	large yellow onion	2	cups beef or chicken stock
½	pound roast meat (beef chuck) or chicken, cubed or shredded	1½	tablespoons curry powder
1	tablespoon all vegetable shortening	4	ounces raisins (optional)

Cook diced apples, onions and meat or chicken for 30 minutes in vegetable shortening and vinegar. Add beef or chicken stock. Add curry powder and raisins. Serve over boiled rice garnished with bananas, peanuts, chutney, pineapple or walnuts.

Middle Eastern Skewered Chicken

8 SERVINGS

3 pounds boneless chicken breast, boneless thigh or combination

3 cloves garlic, crushed

1 tablespoon oregano

1 teaspoon mint, or more to taste

½ cup plus 3 tablespoons vegetable oil

½ cup fresh lemon juice
salt and pepper to taste

2 medium onions, quartered

1 red, green and yellow peppers, seeded and cut in cubes for skewering

Cut chicken into cubes and place in bowl. Add garlic, oregano, mint, ½ cup oil, lemon juice, and pepper to taste. Stir to coat. Cover and refrigerate at least 3 hours. Skewer chicken and season with salt if desired. Set aside. Place onions and peppers in bowl. Add 3 tablespoons oil and season with salt and pepper to taste. Stir to coat and skewer on separate skewers. Grill over high heat, turning often to cook evenly. Serve over rice.

Free Range Roasted Chicken

2 SERVINGS

Free range chickens are raised in an environment where they can roam and graze openly and are leaner than organically and non-organically raised chickens.

1 tablespoon butter

2 tablespoons olive oil

2 pieces free range chicken

Melt butter in a large skillet. Add olive oil and place chicken skin side down. Cook for about 5 minutes on each side. Remove from skillet and place in a shallow baking pan. Roast in oven at 425° for another 10 to 15 minutes (depending upon size of the chicken pieces selected).

Quick and Easy Honey Curry Chicken

4 SERVINGS

4	tablespoons butter or margarine	1	teaspoon curry powder
¼	cup Dijon mustard	½	cup honey
1	teaspoon salt	4	boneless chicken breast halves

Preheat oven to 375°. In a 9x9-inch baking dish, melt butter in the oven. When butter is melted, stir in remaining ingredients except chicken. Rinse and pat dry chicken pieces. Dredge chicken in mixture to coat evenly. Place chicken in baking dish and cook uncovered for 25 minutes. Turn once. Serve with rice; pour remaining sauce over top.

Grilled Yogurt-Lime Chicken

6 SERVINGS

6	boneless, skinless chicken breast halves	1	teaspoon fresh ginger, finely chopped
¼	teaspoon salt	1	teaspoon honey
⅛	teaspoon pepper	1	clove garlic, finely chopped
¼	cup plain non-fat yogurt	1	medium lime, halved
1	tablespoon lime juice		

Place chicken in shallow pan. Sprinkle with salt and pepper. Mix yogurt, lime juice, ginger, honey, and garlic. Pour mixture over chicken. Refrigerate for 2 hours to blend flavors. Turn once. Remove from marinade and discard marinade. Place chicken on a medium heated grill. Squeeze juice from lime halves over chicken. Cover and cook for 20 minutes or until juice of chicken is no longer pink. Serve with rice or orzo.

Jerk Chicken

4 SERVINGS

2 tablespoons fresh or dried thyme

½ teaspoon salt

1 teaspoon crushed red pepper

½ teaspoon allspice

½ teaspoon ground ginger

½ teaspoon nutmeg

½ teaspoon cinnamon

1 medium red onion, chopped

2 tablespoons rum

¼ cup molasses

¼ cup lime juice

4 boneless, skinless chicken breast halves

salt and pepper

1 medium yellow bell pepper, cut in ¼ inch strips

½ cup papaya, sliced

½ cup mango, sliced

Pulse spices, onion, rum, molasses and lime juice in a blender until smooth. Place chicken in sealable plastic bag and coat with the spice mixture. Refrigerate for at least 6 hours or overnight. Coat a 9x13-inch baking pan with vegetable spray. Arrange chicken in baking dish and sprinkle with salt and pepper. Reserve extra marinade from bag. Bake chicken at 350° for 50 to 60 minutes. While chicken is baking, simmer marinade in a small sauce pan. Serve as a sauce on cooked chicken. Chicken is done when juices no longer are pink. Let stand for 15 minutes before serving, tenting with aluminum foil to keep warm or place in warming drawer. Garnish with sliced peppers, papaya and mango. Serve with black or red beans and/or rice.

May also prepare on a medium hot grill. Chicken is cooked when meat thermometer reads 165-170° for breast meat and 180-185° for thigh meat.

Turkey London Broil

1 butterflied boneless turkey breast

1 (8 ounce) bottle Caesar salad dressing, (not creamy type)

In a sealable plastic bag, marinate turkey breast for at least 1 hour or overnight in half of salad dressing. Grill on medium high heat. Baste faithfully with marinade from bag every 10 minutes. Check for doneness at thickest part in 30 minutes. Remove from grill and let rest on platter. Slice thinly against the grain. Top with unused salad dressing, if desired.

1732

Fish House Punch is a strong, rum-based cocktail containing Cognac, peach brandy and diluted with cold, black tea. It was first concocted in 1732 at Philadelphia's fishing club, the Colony in Schuylkill, a.k.a. the "Fish House".

Turkey Burgers

6-8 BURGERS

1½	pounds ground turkey	dash garlic powder
1	egg yolk	salt
2	teaspoons onion, chopped	pepper
½	teaspoon ground mustard	steak seasoning
2	tablespoons barbecue sauce	

Mix all ingredients and form into patties. Broil or grill.

Serve on a sesame seed bun with a slice of tomato. Delicious!

Turkey Pastrami Reuben Sandwiches

2 SERVINGS

4	slices rye bread	2	ounces reduced fat-shredded mozzarella cheese
6	teaspoons light margarine		Thousand Island Dressing
4	ounces turkey pastrami, sliced		
½	cup sauerkraut, drained		

Spread dressing onto one side of each slice of bread. Spread 1 teaspoon of margarine onto the other side. Put half of the pastrami, sauerkraut and mozzarella cheese onto the dressing side of bread. Top with other piece of bread, dressing side in. In a nonstick frying pan or griddle, melt 2 teaspoons of margarine. Grill the sandwiches until golden, 4 minutes on each side. Cut in half and serve. Garnish with spicy mustard and kosher dill pickle.

Vegetarian

Ricotta and Tomato Sformato, recipe page 125

Ricotta and Tomato Sformato *(pictured)*

4 SERVINGS

A soufflé like dish, sformato usually contains vegetables and is baked in ramekins. A ceramic baking dish or a glass, ovenproof baking pan may also be used. Sformato makes a wonderful lunch served with black olives and a green salad.

1 cup cherry tomatoes, stemmed and halved	¾ cup Parmigiano-Reggiano cheese
1 tablespoon unsalted butter at room temperature	2 large eggs
2-3 tablespoons plain, fine dried breadcrumbs	2½ teaspoons fresh, chopped thyme
2 cups whole-milk ricotta cheese	sea salt and freshly ground pepper to taste
	black olives

Position a rack in the middle of the oven and preheat to 350°. Lightly brush rimmed baking sheet with oil. Gently squeeze the tomato halves to extract the seeds and juice. Place tomatoes, cut side up, on the prepared baking sheet and bake 15 to 20 minutes until tomatoes are wrinkled. Remove from oven and let cool slightly. Leave oven on. With butter, generously grease an 8 inch baking dish. Sprinkle the dish with breadcrumbs and tap out the excess. In a medium bowl, whisk together ricotta and Parmigiano-Reggiano cheeses, about ½ of the chopped thyme, and the eggs. Season with salt and pepper. Stir in half of the tomatoes. Using a rubber spatula scrape the mixture into prepared dish and smooth the top. Top with remaining tomato halves, cut side down, then sprinkle with the remaining thyme. Bake 35 to 40 minutes. When the Sformato is done, it will be set around the edges but slightly soft in the center. Remove from the oven and cool a bit (about 10 minutes). Run a knife around the inside edge of the dish to loosen the sides. Serve warm.

Oregano or basil may be used in place of thyme.

Activities in the early years of the Women's Auxiliary revolved around supplying food for doctors and nurses in training, providing support and care for expecting mothers, and contributing funds to cover expenses of running the hospital wards and purchasing hospital equipment.

Vegetarian

1912

The Whitman Sampler was introduced by Philadelphia's Whitman Chocolate Company.

Moroccan Vegetable Stew

4 SERVINGS

1 tablespoon olive oil
1 onion, sliced
½ teaspoon ground coriander
¼ teaspoon turmeric
½ teaspoon cinnamon
½ teaspoon ground ginger
¼ teaspoon cumin
2 tomatoes, chopped

1 medium to large sweet potato, peeled and cut into chunks
¼ cup water
2 tablespoons lemon juice
¾ cup canned garbanzo beans, drained
1 zucchini, cut into 1 inch chunks
½ cup fresh parsley, chopped
¼ cup golden or brown raisins

Heat oil in a large pot or deep skillet. Brown onion until tender. Add spices and cook for 5 minutes. Add tomatoes, sweet potato, water, and lemon juice. Bring to boil, then reduce heat, cover and simmer about 30 minutes or until sweet potato is tender. Add garbanzo beans, zucchini, parsley and raisins. Cover and simmer another 10 minutes.

Hearty Winter Casserole

6 SERVINGS

This is an old Russian recipe. It is simple, filling and delicious.

1 large head cabbage
4 medium sweet onions

1 cup and 2 tablespoons butter, divided
1 bag extra wide soup noodles

Shred cabbage and onions (separately) with hand grater or in food processor. In a frying pan, melt ½ cup of butter and add cabbage, cooking until browned. In separate frying pan, melt ½ cup butter and add onions, cooking until browned. Boil noodles as directed on package. Drain and add 2 tablespoons of butter. Combine all ingredients and place in crockpot, if desired, keeping on warm until serving.

Vegetarian

Gratin Provençal

8 SERVINGS

To prepare ahead, bring to room temperature before reheating at 325° for about 30 minutes.

6   peeled garlic cloves, 1 split and 5 chopped

¼   cup extra virgin olive oil, plus 2 teaspoons for pan

2   pounds baking potatoes, peeled and thinly sliced

     coarse salt and freshly ground pepper

2-3 teaspoons fresh thyme leaves

1   large onion, thinly sliced

5   medium tomatoes, cored and thinly sliced

⅔   cup white wine

Preheat oven to 400°. Rub bottom of large (about 16x10) porcelain gratin dish or glass casserole with garlic halves. Drizzle dish with 2 teaspoons of oil. Arrange potatoes in single layer in gratin dish. Season with ⅓ of the salt, pepper, thyme and chopped garlic. Arrange sliced onions on top of potatoes and season as before. Arrange tomatoes on top of onions and sprinkle with remaining herbs and seasonings. Pour wine and olive oil over casserole. Cover and bake about 20 minutes; uncover and bake for another hour.

Chicken broth may be substituted for wine.

Summer Couscous

4 SERVINGS

Simple to prepare ... bright and refreshing!

1   cup whole wheat couscous

2   tablespoons olive oil

¼   cup fresh orange juice

1   cucumber, diced

¼   cup currants

1   bunch scallions

¼   cup mint leaves, crushed

1   teaspoon kosher salt

Make couscous according to package directions. Cool to room temperature. Stir in remaining ingredients. Let sit 1 hour to blend flavors.

1940s

The Women's Board was first asked by the Board of Trustees to supply an annual report. Receipts in 1942 were $7,407.

Vegetarian

Caponata Sicilian Style

8-10 SERVINGS

This dish may be served chilled as an antipasto or warm as a side or main dish!

2	(1 pound) eggplants, trimmed and cut into 1 inch cubes (no need to remove the skins)
2	red or yellow bell peppers, seeded and cut in ½ inch squares
2	large yellow onions cut into ½ inch cubes
2	tender inner celery stalks, sliced
2	ripe tomatoes, seeded and chopped
¾	cup pitted and chopped Kalamata olives
⅓	cup golden raisins
2	tablespoons capers, drained and rinsed
1½	tablespoons sugar
1½	tablespoons red wine vinegar sea salt
¼-½	cup sliced almonds, toasted olive oil for frying

Pour olive oil to a depth of ½ inch into a deep, heavy frying pan and place over medium heat until hot and an eggplant cube sizzles on contact. Line a large platter with paper towels. Working in batches, arrange eggplant cubes in the pan in a single layer but do not crowd. Cook, stirring occasionally until egg plant is tender and browned, 7 to 8 minutes. With a slotted spoon, transfer eggplant to paper towel lined platter. Repeat with remaining eggplant. When all of the eggplant is cooked, fry bell peppers in the same way until lightly browned and drain on paper towel lined platter. Finally, fry onions and celery together until tender and golden and drain on paper towels.

In a large saucepan, over low heat, combine tomatoes, olives, raisins, capers, sugar and vinegar. Stir well and add fried vegetables and a pinch of salt. Partially cover and cook for about 20 minutes, stirring occasionally, until the mixture thickens. Add a little water if the mixture becomes dry.

Remove from heat and transfer to serving dish cooling to room temperature. If time permits, cover and refrigerate overnight to let the flavors marry. Bring to room temperature before serving and sprinkle almonds over top. Serve at room temperature with thin slices of crusty bread or Melba rounds or warm and serve as a side dish.

Vegetarian

Butternut and Yellow Squash Frittata

Pairs well with a fresh fruit salad.

1	butternut squash, peeled and seeded	4	ounces mozzarella cheese, shredded
1	tablespoon olive oil	1	yellow squash, thinly sliced
1	tablespoon salt		sea salt and pepper
6	eggs		parsley and/or thyme
¼	cup 1% milk		

Chop the butternut squash and put in a roasting pan. Generously coat with olive oil and 1 tablespoon salt. Put into a preheated 350° oven and roast until tender for about 20 minutes.

In a big bowl, combine the eggs and milk. Whisk together until light and airy. Add mozzarella cheese to mixture.

In a 10 inch, nonstick pan, sauté thinly sliced yellow squash with olive oil, salt and pepper for 5 to 10 minutes until tender. Add parsley and/or thyme. Once the roasted butternut squash is tender, add this to the frittata pan with the yellow squash. (Take off the heat to do this.)

Pour the egg mixture over the squash, making sure that the mozzarella cheese gets evenly distributed throughout. Put the pan into the oven for 20 minutes at 350°. You will know it is done when a fork comes out clean — do not overcook!

May use sweet potatoes instead of squash.

1969-1972

Mrs. Dorrance Hamilton served as president. During her term of office, the Women's Board donated $85,000 to build the first heliport in Philadelphia. She reported that the inaugural helicopter ride was the "highlight of her presidency".

Vegetarian

1956

Miss Marion Hayes was appointed as the last Director of the Gray Ladies.

2011

A Tree of Life wall sculpture was hung in the Jefferson Meditation Room in memory of Miss Marion Hayes.

Black Bean and Rice Salad
6 SERVINGS

½ cup olive oil
¼ cup apple cider vinegar
1 tablespoon Dijon mustard
1 teaspoon ground cumin
1 teaspoon minced garlic
2½ cups cooked rice, cooled

15 ounces black beans, drained and rinsed
1 chopped red pepper
1 chopped yellow or orange pepper
1 cup chopped green onions
salt and pepper

Whisk first 5 ingredients in a small bowl until well blended. Season with salt and pepper. Combine remaining ingredients in a large bowl. Toss with enough dressing to coat and season with salt and pepper. Cover and refrigerate.

Substitute rice with quinoa for those on a low carbohydrate diet.

Mexican Spiced Vegetarian Chili
6 SERVINGS

Great served over brown rice. Freezes beautifully!

3 medium onions, chopped
3 red peppers, chopped
2 tablespoons vegetable oil
1 tablespoon mustard seed
1 tablespoon chili powder
1 teaspoon cumin seed

¼ teaspoon cinnamon
1 tablespoon cocoa powder
1 (28 ounce) can whole tomatoes
1 (6 ounce) can tomato paste
2 cans kidney beans with liquid reserved
1 can black beans

Heat oil in a 5 quart pot, add onions and peppers, cooking until onions are translucent. Add mustard seeds and cook for 1 minute. Add chili powder, cumin seed, cinnamon, cocoa and stir for 1 minute. Add tomatoes (breaking up with spoon), tomato paste and 3 cans of beans with liquid. Cook over low heat for 30 minutes, stirring occasionally.

Vegetarian

Chana Masala

4 SERVINGS

This Indian dish is traditionally served in a bowl lined with tomato slices and raw onion slivers, served with Indian bread or rice.

4	tablespoons vegetable oil	1	piece ginger, about ½ inch square, grated
¼	teaspoon whole cumin seeds	1½	tablespoons tomato paste
1	medium sized onion, peeled and finely chopped	20	ounce can chick-peas or garbanzo beans, half of the liquid drained
¼	teaspoon ground cinnamon		
¼	teaspoon nutmeg	½	teaspoon salt
¼	teaspoon ground cloves	⅛-¼	teaspoon cayenne pepper (optional)
1	teaspoon ground coriander		
2	cloves garlic, peeled and minced	1	teaspoon lemon juice

Heat oil in a heavy 10 inch skillet over medium heat. When hot, put in cumin seeds. As they begin to darken, add chopped onions. Stir-fry for about 7 to 8 minutes, until they turn light brown. Lower heat, add cinnamon, nutmeg, cloves and coriander. Mix and add garlic and ginger. Stir-fry for 2 to 3 minutes. Add tomato paste. Add chick-peas/garbanzos. Add salt, cayenne and lemon juice. Stir gently.

Tofu Almond Cheesecake

8-10 SERVINGS

This vegetarian dessert has great almond flavor!

9	ounces firm tofu, drained and sliced	2	tablespoons flour
½	cup part-skim ricotta cheese	1	teaspoon vanilla extract
6	egg whites or 3 eggs	1½	teaspoons almond extract
		4	teaspoons sugar

Blend all ingredients together until smooth. Pour into a pie pan, greased with cooking spray. Bake at 350° for 25 minutes. Chill until cool.

Garnish with slivered almonds. May replace almond extract with other flavored extracts.

2012

The Philadelphia Restaurant, "Vetri," a finalist for the 2012 James Beard Foundation Outstanding Restaurant Award, is called "Possibly the best Italian restaurant on the East Coast".

Vegetarian

1874

The Philadelphia painter, Thomas Eakins studied anatomy at Jefferson under Drs. William Henry Pancoast and his father, Joseph Pancoast, the Professor of Anatomy.

Polenta Casserole
4-6 SERVINGS

¾ cup fresh cilantro

2 (4 ounce) cans diced green chilies, drained

¼ cup canned salsa verde (tomatillo)

3 large garlic cloves, minced

1½ teaspoons ground cumin

1 (16 ounce) polenta (comes in a tube, ready made)

½ cup whipping cream

1 (15 ounce) can black beans, well drained

1 (15 ounce) can golden or white hominy, well drained (or broken up into small pieces)

3 cups (10 ounces) coarsely ground Monterey Jack cheese

Preheat oven to 450°. Oil an 11x7x2-inch glass baking dish. Mix ½ cup cilantro, chilies, salsa, garlic and cumin in a bowl. Slice polenta into 18 (1 inch) rounds. Arrange 9 rounds of polenta on bottom of baking dish and drizzle with cream. Top with ½ beans, ½ hominy, ½ salsa mix and 1½ cups cheese and repeat layering. Cover with foil and bake for 20 minutes. Increase oven temperature to 475°, uncover and bake until top is golden. Remove from oven. Let stand for 5 minutes, sprinkle with remaining cilantro and serve.

Vegetarian Chili
6 SERVINGS

Preparation time: 45 minutes

1 tablespoon cumin seeds

¼ teaspoon cayenne pepper

2 teaspoons paprika

1 teaspoon oregano

2 tablespoons vegetable oil

1 medium onion, chopped

1 green pepper, chopped

4 garlic cloves, minced

1 can black beans

1 can pinto beans

1 (28 ounce) can crushed tomatoes

chipotle pepper

sour cream

cilantro

Toast spices, except garlic, in skillet. Sauté onion and pepper in oil until soft. Add garlic and toasted spices and cook 3 minutes more. Add beans and tomatoes. Cover with water. Simmer for 30 minutes. Season with chipotle pepper and serve with sour cream on side and garnish with cilantro.

South-of-the Border Quinoa Salad

Can be made a day ahead of serving.

DRESSING

5	tablespoons fresh lime juice	1½-2	teaspoons cumin
1	teaspoon salt	⅓	cup extra virgin olive oil

SALAD

1½	cups water	1	green bell pepper
1½	cups quinoa	1	red bell pepper
1½	tablespoons red wine vinegar	1	pint grape or cherry tomatoes, sliced in half
1	(15 ounce) can black beans, rinsed and drained	1	bunch fresh cilantro, stemmed and roughly chopped (not dried)
	salt and pepper to taste		
1½	cups frozen corn kernels, defrosted	8	ounces feta cheese (1-1½ cups)

Dressing: Combine all dressing ingredients. Set aside.

Salad: In a small saucepan, bring 1½ cups water to a boil. Rinse the quinoa in a sieve and add to boiling water. Cook for 10 minutes, then cover and remove from heat. Let quinoa rest for another 10 minutes or more until all water has been absorbed, then fluff with a fork. (Quinoa may be sticky but should not be soggy.) In a large bowl, combine vinegar with the black beans and season with salt and pepper. Mix in the corn, peppers, tomatoes and ⅔ of cilantro. Add the cooked quinoa and mix to combine. Add the dressing and remaining cilantro; toss well. Add feta cheese last and toss again to combine.

May use couscous instead of quinoa.

133

1899

Dante and Luigi's Boarding House and Restaurant opens in South Philadelphia and continues in operation today.

Vegetarian

Vegetarian

Indian Tofu with Brown Rice and Vegetables

4 SERVINGS

2	tablespoons olive oil	1	teaspoon salt
4	large garlic cloves, minced	1	tablespoon red pepper paste
1	medium onion, finely chopped	1	(8 ounce) can tomato sauce
1	pound extra-firm tofu, drain well and cut into 1 inch slices	1	(15 ounce) can diced tomatoes, drained
½	cup light coconut milk	1½	cups frozen peas, thawed
1	tablespoon cumin	1½	cups chopped carrots
1	teaspoon curry powder	2	cups brown rice, cooked
1½	teaspoons ground ginger		

Prepare brown rice according to directions on package. Heat olive oil in a large skillet over medium heat. Add garlic, onion and tofu. Cover and cook, stirring occasionally for 5 to 10 minutes. Add coconut milk, cumin, curry powder, ginger, salt and red pepper paste and bring to a simmer. Add tomato sauce, diced tomatoes, peas and carrots. Simmer, covered for 30 minutes. Serve over rice.

Romanian Chopped Eggplant Salad

6-8 SERVINGS

1	large eggplant	2	tablespoons canola or sunflower oil
3	scallions or medium shallot		salt and pepper to taste
1	small plum tomato		

Place whole eggplant (puncture skin in several places to allow steam to escape) under broiler until very soft to touch. Peel and chop. Lightly sauté scallions (or shallots) and tomato in 1 teaspoon oil. Combine all ingredients and add remaining oil. Serve cold on crackers, black bread or pita.

Vegetable Lasagna

12 lasagna noodles

⅓ cup olive oil

1 large onion, chopped

1 cup large fresh mushrooms, sliced

1 pound can Italian tomatoes

1 (8 ounce) jar tomato sauce

½ cup dry red wine

1 large shredded carrot

1 package frozen chopped spinach, thawed and squeeze out water

2 cloves garlic, pressed

¼ cup fresh parsley

2 tablespoons oregano

2 teaspoons fresh basil leaves, chopped

2 cups part-skim ricotta cheese

1½ cups grated or shredded Parmesan cheese

Cook and drain noodles. Heat oil and sauté onions and mushrooms. Add tomatoes and liquid, tomato sauce, wine, carrot, spinach, garlic, parsley, oregano, and basil. Simmer covered mixture in a large skillet for 30 minutes. Uncover and simmer until sauce is thick. Butter a 9x13-inch pan. Spread ¼ sauce mixture on bottom of pan. Cover with ⅓ of noodles. Dot with ricotta cheese. Sprinkle mozzarella and Parmesan cheeses over layer. Repeat layers 2 times. Spread remaining sauce mixture on top. Sprinkle with Parmesan cheese. Bake at 350° for 40 to 50 minutes. Let stand for 10 minutes before cutting.

1987

The Women's Forum was started in 1987 by JMC'80 grads, Drs. Marianne Ritchey and Barbara Friedman to give aspiring medical students (both men and women) an opportunity to meet and discuss issues related to careers in medicine with a panel of seasoned physicians.

Vegetarian

Eggplant Parmesan

4-5 SERVINGS

A memorable eggplant Parmesan.

EGGPLANT

½ cup all-purpose flour

2 eggs, beaten

1½ cups breadcrumbs

½ tablespoon garlic powder

½ tablespoon minced fresh oregano

2 small eggplants (1 pound each), peeled and cut lengthwise into ½ inch slices

½ cup olive oil

CHEESE

1 egg, beaten

15 ounces ricotta cheese

¾ cup shredded Parmesan cheese, divided

¼ cup thinly sliced fresh basil leaves

¼ teaspoon black pepper

1 (32 ounce) jar puttanesca sauce

4 cups shredded mozzarella cheese, divided

Eggplant: Place flour and eggs in a separate bowls. On a plate, mix breadcrumbs, garlic powder and oregano. Dip eggplant in flour, then in beaten egg and coat with breadcrumb mixture on each side.

Cheese: In a large bowl, combine egg, ricotta cheese, ½ cup Parmesan cheese, basil and pepper. In a 9x13-inch greased pan, layer 1½ cups puttanesca sauce, 4 eggplant slices, 1 cup ricotta mixture and 2 cups mozzarella cheese. Repeat layers once. Sprinkle with remaining Parmesan cheese. Bake at 350° for 35 to 40 minutes. Let stand for 15 minutes before cutting.

Pasta & Rice

Chutney Rice, recipe page 140

2007 – 100 Year Celebration

The Women's Board
of
Thomas Jefferson University Hospital
requests the honor of your presence
at a
Reception

TO CELEBRATE 100 YEARS

of dedication, service and contributions to the hospital

Thursday, June 7, 2007
4 to 6 o'clock
at the home of
Mrs. Samuel M.V. Hamilton
218 Strafford Avenue
Wayne, Pennsylvania

Honorary chair - Mrs. Samuel M.V. Hamilton
Co-chairs - Mrs. Michael J. Vergare and Mrs. James W. Fox IV

Coconut Mango Rice

5-6 SERVINGS

1 tablespoon olive oil	⅔ cup water
1½ cups long-grain rice	1 teaspoon salt
1 (14 ounce) can unsweetened coconut milk	1 large fresh mango, peeled and cubed

In a large saucepan, heat oil over medium heat. Add rice and stir to coat with oil. Add coconut milk, water, and salt. Bring to boil and simmer until liquid is absorbed. Remove rice from heat and fluff with a fork. Place clean, dry dish towel over pan. Cover with lid and let steam for 5 minutes. Add mango before serving.

May be made using frozen mango.

Traditional Risotto

4 SERVINGS

2 tablespoons butter	3 cups chicken broth, heated
2 tablespoons olive oil	1 tablespoon butter
½ cup onion, chopped	3 tablespoons Parmesan cheese, grated
1 cup Arborio rice	
¼ cup white wine	

Melt butter and olive oil together. Sauté onion. Add rice and stir about 2 minutes. Add white wine. After about 1 minute, stir in 1 cup hot broth. Cook and stir until liquid is absorbed. Continue adding broth, stirring until liquid is absorbed. Add 1 tablespoon butter and 3 tablespoons Parmesan cheese and stir.

Delicious when tossed with baby spinach leaves.

1888

Mr. Joseph Horn and Mr. Frank Hardart launch their restaurant empire in a tiny 15 stool lunchroom in central Philadelphia with $1,000 borrowed from a family member and a recipe for coffee. The restaurant was successful and the Horn and Hardart Baking Company operated several lunchrooms throughout Philly.

2008

After existing as a solo storefront in Philadelphia's famed Italian Market for 69 years, DiBruno's Market opens a 10,000 sq. ft., $4 million satellite store in Center City Philadelphia to immediate success. The new location features expanded gourmet offerings and competes successfully against national chains.

Chutney Rice *(pictured)*

12-18 SERVINGS

Should be prepared ahead.

1½	cups chutney	2½	cups chopped apples
½	cup vegetable oil	2½	cups chopped celery
3	tablespoons lemon juice	¾	cup golden raisins
½	teaspoon ground ginger	½	cup chopped, toasted almonds
6	cups rice, cooked and cooled		

Combine chutney, oil, lemon juice and ginger in a large bowl. Stir in remaining ingredients. Refrigerate, covered 2 to 3 hours to blend ingredients.

Wild Rice Casserole

6-8 SERVINGS

1	cup wild rice, soak overnight in bowl covered with water	½	pound fresh mushrooms, sliced
6	slices bacon, fried until crispy	1	cup chicken broth
1	small onion, diced thinly	1	(10½ ounce) can cream of chicken soup
1	small green pepper, diced		salt and pepper to taste
2	ribs celery, diced		sprinkle of paprika

Pour water off wild rice and boil in a large pot of fresh, salted water until fluffy. Drain. Fry bacon until crispy. Blot with paper towel. When bacon is cool, break it into small pieces. Sauté onions, green pepper, and celery until translucent; add sliced mushrooms near end to keep fresh. Put drained wild rice in a bowl and add chicken stock and cream of chicken soup. Mix well. Add onion mixture, bits of bacon and mix well. Salt and pepper to taste. Place mixture into a buttered medium casserole dish. Sprinkle paprika on top. Bake covered at 350° for 25 minutes; continue baking uncovered for 10 minutes.

Add garlic powder or curry powder for a different flavor.

Shrimp Rice Casserole

2	packages frozen spinach, defrosted	1	small jar Cheese-Whiz™	
2	pounds cooked medium shrimp	1	teaspoon salt	
2	cups cooked white rice	1	can sliced water chestnuts, drained	
2	cans cream of celery soup, non-fat, low sodium			

Squeeze out excess moisture from thawed spinach. Combine all ingredients, mix well. Turn into casserole dish. Bake at 350° for 30 minutes.

Orzo Chicken

1	tablespoon olive oil	1½	cups water	
1	cup onion, diced	8	chicken tenders	
1	cup carrots, shredded	4	cups chunky tomato sauce	
2	tablespoons garlic, minced	4	ounces orzo	
1	cup flour	10	ounces baby spinach	
1	tablespoon Italian seasoning	½	cup mozzarella cheese, shredded	

Sauté onion, carrot and garlic in olive oil over medium heat in a large skillet. Cook until soft (5 minutes). Remove vegetables and set aside. Combine flour and seasoning. Coat chicken in flour mixture. Brown chicken (5 minutes). Add ½ cup water to deglaze the skillet. Add tomato sauce to pan, and then add cooked vegetables. Cover and simmer for 25 to 30 minutes. Add orzo and 1 cup water. Cook 4 to 5 minutes. Sprinkle spinach and mozzarella cheese on top. Cover and cook 5 minutes.

May substitute grano for orzo just after sauce is added. Add 1 additional cup of water. Cover and simmer for 25 to 30 minutes.

1961

The Pennywise Thrift Shop, a Women's Board venture, opened its doors in Ardmore, PA. In 2011 the Pennywise, which has raised over $3 million to support patient care at Thomas Jefferson University Hospital, celebrated its 50th anniversary.

Sardinian Lasagna

MEAT SAUCE

½ pound lean ground beef

1 pound Italian sausage

2 (16 ounce) cans Italian plum tomatoes with basil

2 teaspoons dried crushed basil

1 (10¾ ounce) can tomato sauce

1 teaspoon salt

1 teaspoon sugar

1 tablespoon fresh or minced garlic

CHEESE FILLING

3 eggs, beaten

1 cup whole or part-skim ricotta cheese

1 cup dry cottage cheese

⅔ cup grated Parmesan/Romano cheese

¼ cup minced fresh parsley

salt to taste

½ teaspoon fresh ground pepper

NOODLES

8 ounces lasagna noodles

1 (12 ounce) package sliced mozzarella cheese slices

Prepare meat sauce by browning ground beef and sausage, then adding other ingredients. Simmer 30 minutes. Cook lasagna noodles, set aside in cool water. Separate mozzarella cheese slices. Prepare cheese filling. To assemble: spread thin layer of meat sauce in bottom of greased 9x13-inch baking dish. Layer ½ lasagna noodles over sauce. Cover with ½ cheese filling; half of remaining meat sauce, ½ mozzarella cheese slices. Repeat layers, adding last of mozzarella cheese slices on top. Bake in preheated 375° oven for 30 to 40 minutes. Let lasagna stand for 10 minutes before cutting into pieces. Serve with grated Parmesan cheese and crunchy garlic toast.

Magnificent Manicotti

FILLING

2	pounds ricotta cheese	3	tablespoons flat leaf parsley, chopped
¼	cup mozzarella cheese, grated	2	eggs

CRÊPES

3	eggs	1	cup flour
½	cup milk	¼	teaspoon salt
½	cup water	1	cup tomato sauce
3	tablespoons butter, melted	2-3	tablespoons mozzarella, shredded

Filling: Mix ricotta cheese, mozzarella cheese, parsley and eggs; refrigerate overnight.

Crêpes: Combine eggs, milk, water, butter, flour and salt in a blender. Blend about 1 minute. Scrape down sides. Blend about 30 seconds. Refrigerate for 1 hour. Brush a 6 inch crêpe pan with melted butter. Heat and add just enough batter to cover bottom of the pan, tilting from side to side to distribute evenly. Cook until the shine on top of crêpe dulls. Flip and cook for 3 to 4 seconds, repeating until all crêpes are made.

Fill crêpes by placing about 2 tablespoons of filling mixture down the center of each. Fold right side over and tuck. Fold left side over and place seam side down in a 9x13-inch pan that has a thin layer of tomato sauce in the bottom and up the sides. Repeat until completed. Spoon tomato sauce over the top of manicotti. Sprinkle 2 to 3 tablespoons of mozzarella over the top. Cover with foil and bake in a 325° oven for 30 minutes.

1902

The very first Horn & Hardart automat opened at 1818 Chestnut St, Philadelphia.

My Mother-in-Law's Penne with Pesto Sauce

4-6 SERVINGS

2 cloves garlic, minced	3 ounces vodka
1-2 shallots, minced	16 ounces heavy cream
2 tablespoons extra virgin olive oil	⅓ cup melted butter
2 tablespoons tomato pesto	1 cup Romano cheese
14 ounces tomato sauce	1 pound penne pasta

Sauté garlic, shallots and tomato pesto in olive oil. Add tomato sauce and vodka and cook until heated. Add heavy cream, butter and Romano cheese to sauce and cook until thickened. Cook and strain pasta. Ladle sauce over pasta and serve.

May substitute traditional pesto for tomato pesto.

Lasagna al Pesto

6 SERVINGS

oil for baking pan	½ teaspoon salt
16 lasagna noodles	pepper, to taste
1 pound fresh spinach	¾ cup grated Parmesan cheese
2 pounds ricotta cheese	⅓ cup toasted pine nuts
1 cup pesto	1 pound grated mozzarella
4 cloves garlic, minced	

Preheat oven to 350°. Lightly oil a 9x13-inch baking pan. Cook noodles. Mince spinach. Combine ricotta, spinach, pesto, garlic, salt, pepper, ½ cup Parmesan in a large bowl and mix. Place a layer of noodles in the bottom of the baking pan. Spoon ⅓ of filling over the noodles, sprinkle ⅓ of the mozzarella on top. Repeat twice. Top with a layer of noodles. Sprinkle remaining Parmesan on top. Bake for 50 minutes (if top browns too quickly cover loosely with foil).

Use two packages of frozen chopped spinach, thawed and drained instead of fresh.

Not-the-Usual Mac and Cheese 6 SERVINGS

2½ cups macaroni, cooked according to the package directions

1 can mushroom soup

1 (6½ ounce) can mushrooms, drained (optional)

1 cup mayonnaise

1 pound grated Cheddar cheese

¼ cup chopped onion

¼ cup chopped green pepper

¼ cup chopped pimento

3 tablespoons melted butted

18 round buttery crackers, crumbled

Combine ingredients from macaroni through pimento in a 9x13-inch pan, sprayed with non-stick spray. Top with 3 tablespoons of butter combined with cracker crumbs. Bake at 375° for 25 to 30 minutes.

Penne with Turkey Sausage and Sun-Dried Tomatoes 4-6 SERVINGS

1 pound penne

2 tablespoons olive oil

1½ pounds turkey Italian sausage

3 garlic cloves, minced

2 cups chicken broth

1 cup white wine

½ cup sun-dried tomatoes, thinly sliced

2 tablespoons capers

¼ cup Parmesan cheese, grated

Bring large pot of salted water to a boil. Add the penne and cook according to the package directions. Drain. In a large sauté pan, heat 2 tablespoons of oil over medium high heat. Add turkey sausage and cook until golden brown (about 10 minutes). Transfer the sausage to a plate and slice sausage into circles. In the same sauté pan, add garlic and sauté for 30 seconds. Add white wine, chicken broth, sun-dried tomatoes, capers and cooked, sliced sausage into the pan. Bring mixture to a boil, then reduce to a simmer and cook for 15 minutes. Season with salt and pepper to taste. Add pasta to sauté pan and toss. Transfer to large serving bowl and sprinkle cheese on top.

Miss Ella Benson was the first Directress of Nurses at Jefferson and was in charge of teaching the student nurses along with members of the Attending Medical Staff. Within months of opening the School of Nursing and having student nurses on the wards, the improvement in the care of patients was obvious.

1876

Raggio and Guano's macaroni factory founded at Seventh and Montrose Streets was one of the first pasta factories in the U.S.

Ricotta Cheese Gnocchi

4-6 SERVINGS

2	eggs	1	cup flour
½	teaspoon salt	1	pound whole milk ricotta cheese
	dash pepper	¼	cup Parmesan cheese

Bring small pot of water to a boil and salt. In a large bowl, mix eggs, salt and pepper. Add flour and mix until well blended. Whisk in ricotta cheese until smooth. Place a spoonful of dough into the boiling water to make sure that it will hold its shape. If it does not, stir in additional flour until it does. Divide the dough into 3 or 4 pieces and roll into ½ inch round ropes on a floured surface. Cut each rope into 1 inch pieces and place on a lightly floured baking sheet. Run the backside of a fork over each piece to create a design. Place in refrigerator until ready to use. When ready to use bring a large pot of water to a boil. Boil gnocchi until they float to the surface, about 1 to 2 minutes. Drain and serve with Parmesan cheese and homemade Marinara Sauce, page 190.

Fettuccine Alfredo (with Chicken & Broccoli)

4 SERVINGS

1	pound chicken	1	medium head of broccoli
1	teaspoon olive oil	1	teaspoon salt
1	pound fettuccine pasta		freshly ground pepper
1-1½	cups Parmesan cheese, grated		
1	cup heavy cream		

Cook chicken in large skillet with olive oil, drain. Cut into small pieces or shred. In a separate pot, cook pasta in a large quantity of 8 quarts salted boiling water until al dente. Drain well. Add Parmesan cheese and heavy cream to pasta a little at a time. Toss gently. Add broccoli and chicken. Mix slightly and serve immediately. Season with freshly ground pepper.

Shrimp may be used instead of chicken.

Pennsylvania Dutch Macaroni and Cheese

4-6 SERVINGS

This may be made a day ahead and kept in a refrigerator, tightly covered, baking until bubbly!

8	ounces elbow macaroni	¼	teaspoon dry mustard
2	tablespoons butter	2	cups shredded extra sharp white Cheddar cheese
2	tablespoons flour		grated Parmesan cheese or breadcrumbs for top
2½	cups skim milk		
1	teaspoon salt		

Cook macaroni as instructed reducing time to 7 minutes then drain. (For best results macaroni should be firm, not completely cooked.) Do not rinse. Melt butter and blend in flour. Gradually stir in milk and seasonings. Cook and stir over low to medium heat until smooth and thickened. Mix macaroni, sauce and shredded cheese. Pour into a greased 2 quart casserole. Sprinkle top with breadcrumbs or cheese. Bake at 350° for 30 minutes.

Audrey's Famous Noodle Ring

1	pound medium egg noodles	4	eggs, separated
½	pint sour cream	1	tablespoon plain breadcrumbs for topping
½	pound cream cheese		
½	pound butter		

Boil and drain noodles. Add sour cream, cream cheese, butter, and egg yolks. Beat egg whites and fold into mixture. Butter a large ring mold and dust with breadcrumbs. (Can also be baked in a large casserole dish.) Bake at 350° for 40 minutes. Cool slightly and flip onto serving platter.

Use as a side dish instead of potatoes.

1950

Stromboli was invented by Nazzareno Romano at Romano's Italian Restaurant & Pizzeria, in Essington, Tinicum Township, just outside of Philadelphia. It was named after the movie Stromboli, *starring Ingrid Bergman.*

1839

Joseph Pancoast, MD, Professor of Surgery from 1839 to 1841 and of Anatomy from 1841 to 1874, wrote extensively on operations for diseases of the bones and joints in his textbook, Operative Surgery *(1844).*

Apple Kugel

8 SERVINGS

1	pound fine noodles	1	teaspoon cinnamon
1	stick margarine, melted	½	box golden raisins
4	eggs, separated	1	cup cornflakes, crushed
5	apples, sliced thin	½	stick margarine, melted
1½	cups sugar (less 2 tablespoons)		

Cook, rinse and drain noodles. Add margarine to noodles. Beat egg yolks and add to noodle. Add sugar, cinnamon and raisins. Add apples. Pour into a greased 9x13-inch pan. Mix cornflakes with margarine and place on top of noodles. Bake in a 350° oven for 30 to 45 minutes.

Asian Noodle Toss

6 SERVINGS

Can make a day ahead of serving.

NOODLES

2	packages Ramen Oriental flavor noodle soup	3-4	scallions, sliced into ¼ inch pieces
2	cups shredded raw cabbage (white or red)	¾	cup slivered almonds

DRESSING

3	tablespoons white sugar	2	packs of seasoning from noodle soup
⅔	cup vegetable oil	½	teaspoon salt
1	teaspoon sesame oil	3	tablespoons rice vinegar

Noodles: Break up Ramen noodles and cook according to package directions. Combine hot, drained noodles with cabbage, scallions, and almonds in a bowl. Dressing: Mix all dressing ingredients together and pour ¾ of dressing over noodles and toss. Refrigerate for at least 4 hours or overnight. When ready to serve, toss and taste. Add rest of dressing if needed.

Use Splenda in place of sugar. May add cut up chicken or shrimp.

Vegetables

Roasted Garden Vegetables, recipe page 151

1968 – Pennywise Thrift Shop Mortgage Burning Party

Mrs. Samuel Hamilton,
Mrs. Calvin Rankin,
Mrs. Frank Fogarty,
and Jane Tren.

Citrus Roasted Asparagus

4 SERVINGS

Good served cold or at room temperature for a picnic or buffet.

1	pound medium-thick asparagus (12 to 14 spears), trimmed		Kosher salt
2	tablespoons olive oil		freshly ground black pepper
2	tablespoons fresh lemon juice	1-2	tablespoons chopped fresh dill

Preheat oven to 425°. Place asparagus on baking sheet in one layer. Drizzle with oil and lemon juice, and sprinkle with salt and pepper; toss to coat. Roast for 15 minutes, stirring occasionally, until crisp-tender. Toss with dill and serve.

Roasted Garden Vegetables *(pictured)*

8 SERVINGS

1	medium eggplant (about 1½ pounds), peeled into strips and cut into 1 inch cubes	1	medium green pepper, cored, seeded and cut into 1 inch pieces
1	medium zucchini, halved lengthwise and cut crosswise into ½ inch pieces	1	medium red pepper, cored, seeded and cut into 1 inch pieces
1	medium yellow squash, halved lengthwise and cut crosswise into ½ inch pieces	3	tablespoons olive oil
			salt and pepper to taste
1	medium yellow pepper, cored, seeded and cut into 1 inch pieces	½	cup golden raisins
		3	tablespoons fresh lemon juice
		2	teaspoons fresh lemon zest

In a large bowl, toss vegetables in olive oil. Arrange vegetables in one layer in a large shallow baking pan (a large jelly-roll pan works well); sprinkle with salt and pepper. Bake 30 minutes or until tender, stirring occasionally. Stir in raisins and continue baking another 5 minutes. In a large bowl, toss vegetables with lemon juice and zest. May be served hot or refrigerate and serve chilled or at room temperature.

1914

Amoroso's Bread Bakery outgrew its Camden site and moved across the river to Philadelphia to 6505 Haverford Avenue. Amoroso's Rolls are used by thousands annually for Philly cheesesteaks and hoagies.

The first graduating class of nurses consisted of 5 women: Mary Armstrong, Carrie Bear, Sara Brook Bower, Georgianna Bower and Sara Elizabeth Martin, who received the Training School Diploma. They immediately commenced employment at the Hospital.

Pecan Brussels Sprouts

4-6 SERVINGS

1½ pounds small Brussels sprouts, trimmed and halved

½ cup pecan halves

1 tablespoon olive oil

¾ teaspoon kosher salt

½ teaspoon freshly ground black pepper

1 tablespoon butter

Preheat oven to 375°. Place a 9x13-inch roasting pan in oven to heat. Combine Brussels sprouts, pecans, oil, salt and pepper; carefully add to hot pan. Bake for 25 to 30 minutes until sprouts are crisp and tender, stirring occasionally. Add butter, toss and serve immediately.

Roasted Plum Tomatoes

4-6 SERVINGS

These roasted tomatoes also make a zesty topping for bruschetta or pizza, add great flavor to sandwiches; and along with grated cheese and chopped herbs make for a luscious pasta topper. Also freezes nicely for dreary winter months.

2 pounds plum tomatoes, cut in half lengthwise, cored and seeded

½ cup good quality olive oil

2 medium cloves garlic, chopped

½ teaspoon kosher salt

¼ teaspoon dried oregano leaves, crushed

¼ teaspoon freshly ground black pepper

Preheat oven to 400°. Lay tomatoes, cut side up in a 9x13-inch baking dish; drizzle with oil. Sprinkle remaining ingredients evenly over tomatoes. Roast tomatoes for 30 minutes. Turn temperature down to 300° and bake for at least another hour or until edges are slightly brown and caramelized. Cool slightly; peel off skin. Scrape any browned bits in pan and pour into covered container along with tomatoes. Refrigerate for up to 5 days.

Tuscan Kale Crisps

4-6 SERVINGS

12 large Tuscan kale leaves, rinsed, dried, cut in half with center ribs and stems removed

1 tablespoon olive oil

Kosher salt to taste

Freshly ground black pepper to taste

Preheat oven to 250°. Toss kale with oil, salt and pepper in a large bowl. Arrange leaves in single layer on baking sheets. Bake until crisp–about 30 minutes.

Substitute other type of kale or Swiss chard if Tuscan kale is not available. Curlier leaves will take longer to crisp.

Portabella Mushroom Sauté

4 SERVINGS

Delicious served over pasta or as a side-dish to grilled steaks!

1½ pounds portabella mushrooms, cleaned with stems removed

2 small shallots, peeled and chopped

4 tablespoons unsalted butter

coarse salt to taste (optional)

freshly ground black pepper (optional)

¼ cup balsamic vinegar

2½ tablespoons soy sauce

1½ tablespoons sugar

2 green onions, thinly sliced

Halve portabellas and then cut into ¼ inch slices. In large heavy 12 inch skillet, cook shallots in butter over medium heat for about 1 minute, stirring. Add mushrooms, salt and pepper if desired; cook stirring occasionally, until mushroom liquid evaporates, about 10 minutes. (Mushrooms may be prepared to this point 1 day ahead of time, covered and chilled.) In a small bowl, whisk together vinegar, soy sauce and sugar. Increase heat in skillet to medium-high and add vinegar mixture to mushrooms; boil together 3 minutes until liquid is slightly reduced. Add green onions. Serve immediately.

1998

National Geographic's "Food Journeys of a Lifetime" names Capogiro Gelato Artisans in Philly as the "#1 Coolest Place to Eat Ice Cream".

Marinated Carrots

4-6 SERVINGS

1	pound carrots, peeled and cut in julienne strips
¼	cup olive oil
3	tablespoons red wine vinegar
½-¾	teaspoon dried oregano leaves, crushed
½	teaspoon each salt and freshly ground black pepper
2	medium cloves garlic, very thinly sliced

In a medium saucepan, boil carrots for about 10 minutes or until just tender. Do not overcook. Drain well and place in bowl. Whisk together oil, vinegar, oregano, salt and pepper; stir in garlic. Pour marinade over carrots. Cover and chill for several hours or overnight. Carrots may be gently reheated to serve hot or may be served cold.

Creamy Horseradish Carrot Bake

6-8 SERVINGS

6-8	medium carrots, peeled and cut in ¼ inch slices
½	cup mayonnaise
¼	cup water
2	tablespoons minced onion or dry onion flakes
2	tablespoons prepared horseradish
½	teaspoon salt
¼	teaspoon pepper
¼	cup breadcrumbs
2	teaspoons butter, melted

Preheat oven to 375°. Lightly grease a 1½ quart casserole. Cook carrots in boiling water until tender, about 10 to 15 minutes; drain. In a medium bowl combine next 6 ingredients. Gently toss carrots into mixture; spoon into prepared casserole. Combine breadcrumbs and melted butter; sprinkle over carrot mixture. Bake for 25 minutes or until hot.

Prysnic

May be made night before and reheated.

1	pound cottage cheese	1½	boxes chopped frozen broccoli, thawed
3	eggs		
3	tablespoons flour	4	ounces American cheese, cut in cubes
3	tablespoons butter, cut in cubes		

Preheat oven to 350°. Mix all ingredients in large bowl. Pour into greased casserole dish. Cover and cook for 1 hour and 10 minutes, until hot.

Orange Pecan Sweet Potatoes 10-12 SERVINGS

May be prepared, frozen and reheated. Great to make ahead for Thanksgiving – reheat casserole while carving the turkey!

3	pounds sweet potatoes, peeled and cubed	½	cup orange juice
		1	teaspoon cinnamon
2	eggs	1	teaspoon vanilla
¾	cup packed brown sugar, divided	½	teaspoon ground nutmeg
8	tablespoons butter, divided	1	cup chopped pecans

Preheat oven to 350°. In a large saucepan, cook sweet potatoes in boiling water until tender (about 20 minutes); drain. Mash potatoes, then add eggs, ¼ cup of brown sugar, 4 tablespoons butter, orange juice, cinnamon, vanilla and nutmeg; beat until fluffy. Pour into a 2-quart casserole. Melt remaining 4 tablespoons butter and combine with remaining ½ cup brown sugar; drizzle evenly over casserole. Sprinkle pecans on top. Bake at 375° uncovered for 30 to 40 minutes, or until hot.

1917

The hoagie sandwich was invented in Philadelphia by Italian-American workers at the World War II era shipyard (known as Hog Island). Various sliced meats, cheeses and lettuce were put between two slices of Italian bread. This became known as a "Hoagie".

1942-1947

Mrs. J. Howard Pew served as President and was the first delegate to the newly formed Pennsylvania Association of Hospital Auxiliaries in 1949.

Vegetable Tian

This recipe halves or doubles well. It has lots of "play" so you can try variations to suit your taste.

olive oil spray

3-4 large yellow or Spanish onions, cut in half and thinly sliced

2 tablespoons olive oil, divided

3 cloves garlic, minced

1 pound medium round red or white potatoes, unpeeled

1 pound zucchini

1½ pounds tomatoes

1 tablespoon fresh thyme or 1 teaspoon dried thyme leaves, crushed

½ teaspoon each kosher salt and freshly ground pepper

thyme sprigs, optional

4 ounces Gruyère cheese, grated (about 2 cups)

Preheat oven to 375°. Spray a 9x15x2-inch baking or gratin dish with olive oil spray. In a large sauté pan, cook sliced onions in 1 tablespoon olive oil on medium heat about 10 minutes or until onions are translucent, stirring occasionally. Add garlic and cook another 2 minutes. Spread onion mixture into bottom of prepared baking dish. Thinly slice remaining vegetables. Take one potato slice and place up-right on its edge in the onion mixture, follow with zucchini slice, then tomato slice. Continue alternating vegetables making tightly packed rows to fill baking dish. Sprinkle top with thyme leaves, salt and pepper; drizzle with remaining 1 tablespoon olive oil. Top with thyme sprigs, if desired. Cover with aluminum foil and bake 40 to 60 minutes, until potatoes are tender. Uncover, remove thyme sprigs and sprinkle with cheese. Bake uncovered, another 20 to 30 minutes or until top is browned. Serve warm.

Festive Fall Bake

This recipe was donated by the National Foundation for Celiac Awareness (NFCA) and is gluten free. This is an NFCA staff favorite!

4-5 large apples

1 medium butternut squash, peeled and seeds discarded

2 medium sweet potatoes, peeled

1 tablespoon extra virgin olive oil

cinnamon

nutmeg

½ cup orange juice

Preheat oven to 350°. Cube apples, squash and sweet potatoes; spread in a large roasting pan. Toss with olive oil and sprinkle with cinnamon and nutmeg. Pour orange juice over mixture and toss lightly. Cover with foil and bake for 25 minutes. Remove foil and bake for another 5 to 10 minutes or until fork tender.

Glazed Acorn Squash

2 SERVINGS

This recipe doubles and even triples well!

1 acorn squash (approximately 1¼ pounds)

2 tablespoons chopped walnuts or pecans

1 tablespoon brown sugar, packed

1 teaspoon grated orange or tangerine rind

1½ tablespoons butter, divided

Put whole acorn squash in microwave safe 11x7-inch dish and microwave on high for 2½ minutes. Handling carefully, cut squash in half from stem end to tip. Remove seeds and membrane. In the same baking dish, place squash halves, cut side-down and microwave on high for 3 minutes. In small bowl, mix nuts, brown sugar and rind. Turn squash halves cut-sides up and spoon half of the brown sugar mixture into the center of each half; top each center with butter. Cover with waxed paper and microwave on high for 3 to 4 minutes, until a fork can easily pierce the side of the squash. Spoon a little of the melted butter/brown sugar from the center onto the top edge of each squash half. Let sit for 5 minutes before serving.

Jefferson Jewel

First held in the 1970s, the Jewel was a much anticipated fundraising event for over 20 years. A donated piece of fine jewelry was proffered as a raffle.

Red Cabbage with Apples

8-10 SERVINGS

1	small head red cabbage (about 1½ pounds)	2	Granny Smith apples, cored and cut into ¼ inch slices
4	tablespoons butter	¼	cup apple cider
1	large onion, sliced thin	2	tablespoons balsamic vinegar
1	small clove, garlic, minced	¾	teaspoon salt

Cut cabbage in quarters lengthwise, remove core and cut into 1 inch wide strips. In large skillet or Dutch oven, melt butter, add onion and garlic and sauté on medium heat for 5 minutes or until softened (don't let garlic brown). Add shredded cabbage to skillet and cook until crisp-tender (5 to 10 minutes), stirring occasionally. Add apples to skillet and cook 4 to 5 minutes more or until apples are just tender. Stir in remaining ingredients; season to taste with additional vinegar or salt.

May substitute green cabbage for red.

Beet and Apple Purée

4 CUPS OR 6 SERVINGS

Beautiful color makes this a great side dish for holiday meals. Freezes well and is good hot or cold.

5	medium beets, peeled and diced	1	teaspoon sugar
3	tablespoons unsalted butter	1	teaspoon salt
1	cup chopped onions	2	tablespoons fresh lemon juice
4	apples, peeled, cored and chopped	2	tablespoons prepared horseradish

In a saucepan, cover beets with cold water. Bring to boil, cover and simmer until beets are tender (about 20 minutes). Meanwhile, melt butter in medium saucepan or very large skillet; add onions and cook on medium heat until onions are tender, stirring occasionally. Add apples, sugar, salt and lemon juice and continue cooking for 15 to 10 minutes, or until apples are very tender, stirring occasionally. Drain beets. Spoon drained beets into a food processor or blender and purée; add apple mixture and horseradish and continue blending until smooth. Return purée to saucepan to reheat or cover and refrigerate to serve chilled.

Twice Baked Potatoes

May be made up to a day before serving — fill skins, cover and refrigerate. Before serving bake in a 350° oven for 40 minutes.

4	large baking potatoes
4	ounces low-fat cream cheese
1	stick butter, softened
⅓	cup grated Cheddar cheese, divided

salt and pepper to taste

2-3 tablespoons milk or cream (optional)

Preheat oven to 375°. Scrub potatoes: prick skins with fork and bake for 1 hour or until soft. While still hot, cut each potato in half lengthwise and scoop potato pulp into a medium-sized mixing bowl. Add cream cheese and butter; mash. Blend in about ¼ cup of Cheddar cheese. Season to taste with salt and pepper. If mixture seems dry, add milk, one tablespoon at a time, until desired consistency. Reduce oven temperature to 350°. Fill empty potato skins with potato mixture; sprinkle with remaining Cheddar cheese. Place on baking sheet and heat for 20 minutes or until hot.

Parmesan Potatoes

¼	cup grated Parmesan or Pecorino Romano cheese
¼	cup flour
½	teaspoon salt

freshly ground pepper to taste

5 medium potatoes, peeled and cut into 1 to 1½ inch cubes

¼ cup butter

Preheat oven to 350°. In a gallon size plastic bag, combine cheese, flour, salt and pepper; shake to mix well. Place cubed potatoes in bag; shake bag to thoroughly coat potatoes. In a large pan melt butter. Pour cheese coated potatoes into pan stirring to cover with butter. Arrange potatoes in a single layer. Bake 45 minutes at 350°, stirring occasionally until potatoes are tender, golden and crispy on the outside.

1876

The 1876 Centennial Fair was located along the Schuylkill River in the area known as Fairmont Park. About 9 million visitors attended, which was staggering considering that the total population of the U.S. was 46 million.

Bistro Potatoes

Perfect for entertaining. Make a day ahead of time.

4-5 baking potatoes	salt
1 clove garlic, peeled and sliced in half	pepper
1 pint heavy cream	paprika

The day before serving, bake potatoes halfway (about 30 minutes at 425°). Refrigerate overnight. Next day, preheat oven to 375°. Butter a 9x12-inch glass baking dish; rub bottom and sides with garlic half. Peel and grate potatoes into baking dish. Pour cream evenly over top and sprinkle with salt, pepper and paprika. Bake uncovered about 40 minutes until crisp and golden on top.

Ballymaloe Oven Roasted Vegetables

An Irish country recipe.

1 parsnip	pepper
2 large carrots	fresh rosemary sprigs, chopped
2 sweet potatoes	fresh lemon thyme, leaves
4 fingerling potatoes	fresh flat leaf parsley
4 red or purple new potatoes	fresh chives
1 medium red onion	Kosher salt
3 tablespoons olive oil	freshly ground black pepper

Preheat oven to 200°. Cut parsnip, carrots, potatoes, and onion into cubes. Coat a shallow baking dish, 9x13-inch, with olive oil or olive oil spray. Spread vegetables in a single layer and season well with kosher salt and pepper. Roast, uncovered in preheated 200° oven, stir occasionally until fully cooked and they are just beginning to caramelize, about an hour (take care not burn, as vegetables will become bitter). Serve sprinkled with the freshly chopped herbs.

Vary herbs to suit taste. Excellent roasted in a wood burning oven. Colorful and flavorful.

Baltimore Scalloped Corn Pudding

6-8 SERVINGS

1 can corn (or use fresh corn cut off the cob)

½ cup saltine cracker crumbs

4 tablespoons Cheddar cheese, shredded

1 teaspoon sugar

⅔ cup milk

1 egg, beaten

2 tablespoons butter, melted

Preheat oven to 350°. In a large bowl, thoroughly mix all ingredients, except cheese. Spoon into a buttered casserole dish. Sprinkle with Cheddar cheese. Bake uncovered for 35 minutes, until hot and bubbly.

Asparagus-Proscuitto Wraps

Attractive party veggie.

16 spears medium-thick asparagus rinsed, trimmed, with stem cut diagonally

4 ounces cream cheese, softened

1 teaspoon minced garlic freshly ground black pepper

8 pieces prosciutto (about 4 ounces)

Preheat broiler. Cook asparagus in boiling water for 3 minutes or until bright green. Remove from water and plunge into ice cold water. Drain. In a small bowl, blend cream cheese, minced garlic and a pinch of black pepper. Cut each piece of prosciutto in half, length-wise. Spread each piece of prosciutto with about ¾ teaspoon of the cream cheese mixture; wrap around the middle of the asparagus spear. Place on a cookie sheet and broil until the prosciutto begins to get crispy. Serve with a pasta dish for a main course or as an appetizer.

Cheesy Hash Brown Potato Bake

10-12 SERVINGS

⅓ cup cornflake crumbs

2 tablespoons melted butter

1 large bag frozen hash brown potatoes

1 (10¾ ounce) can cream of chicken soup

1 (10¾ ounce) can cream of potato soup

1 (8 ounce) carton sour cream

1 small onion, chopped

1 green pepper, chopped, optional

2 cups sharp Cheddar cheese

¼ teaspoon garlic powder
  paprika
  parsley

Mix cornflakes with melted butter. Combine all other ingredients and turn into a 9x13-inch pan. Top with cornflake crumb mixture. Sprinkle paprika on top. Bake at 350° for 1½ hours. Garnish with fresh parsley before serving.

Broccoli Puff

6-8 SERVINGS

1 tablespoon butter, melted

2 (10 ounce) packages frozen broccoli

1 cup Bisquick™

1 cup 1% milk

½ teaspoon salt

¼ teaspoon white pepper

2 eggs

4 ounces shredded medium sharp Cheddar cheese

Preheat oven to 350°. Grease soufflé dish with melted butter. Cook frozen broccoli until bright green and still crunchy. Drain well. Combine Bisquick™, milk, salt, pepper and eggs, mixing gently. Pour mixture into soufflé dish and bake for 35 to 40 minutes.

Use corn or spinach in place of broccoli.

Sharyn's Spinach Soufflé

8 SERVINGS

This dish may be prepared in advance.

4   (10 ounce) packages frozen chopped spinach, thaw in colander and press out liquid
1   can cream of mushroom soup
1⅓ cups mayonnaise
5   eggs, slightly beaten
1   cup shredded cheese (Swiss or sharp Cheddar)
    vegetable shortening

Combine all ingredients, except cheese, in a mixing bowl using a whisk or wooden spoon. Coat inside of 1½ quart soufflé dish with vegetable shortening. Press ½ cup of cheese into the sides of dish. Pour spinach mixture into soufflé dish. Sprinkle remaining ½ cup of grated cheese over top of soufflé. Bake for 1 hour at 350°. Soufflé is done when top is browned.

Excellent served as a side dish or a lunch entrée.

Oven Roasted Ratatouille

6-8 SERVINGS

1   medium zucchini, halved lengthwise and cut crosswise into ½ inch pieces
1   medium yellow squash, halved lengthwise and cut crosswise into ½ inch pieces
1   yellow pepper, cut into 1 inch pieces
1   green pepper, cut into 1 inch pieces
1   eggplant, cut into 1 inch pieces
3   tablespoons olive oil
½   cup golden raisins
2   teaspoons fresh lemon zest
    juice of 1 lemon
    salt and pepper to taste

Preheat oven to 450°. In a large bowl, toss vegetables in olive oil with salt and pepper. Arrange in one layer on a jelly-roll baking pan. Roast, stirring occasionally until tender, about 30 minutes. Stir in raisins and roast another 5 minutes. Place on a serving plate and top with lemon zest and lemon juice.

Delicious served with yellow saffron rice.

Scalloped Asparagus Casserole   3 SERVINGS

This recipe came to us from the 1960 Jefferson Nurses Alumnae cookbook entitled, "Favorite Recipes Submitted by the School of Nursing of the Jefferson Medical College Hospital" (Julia Tyler Gaskill, Ed.). The original recipe was from Hannah E. Wertman Umpstead, Class of 1928.

WHITE SAUCE

2	tablespoons butter	¼	teaspoon salt
2	tablespoons flour		dash of pepper
1	cup milk	½	cup sharp Cheddar cheese, diced

CASSEROLE

2   tablespoons butter

⅓   cup breadcrumbs

½   bunch (about a ½ pound) fresh asparagus, (rinse, trim ends and chop into 1-inch pieces), then steam

2   hard-boiled eggs, (prepared ahead), chopped

Preheat oven to 375°.

White Sauce: Melt butter in saucepan over low heat. Whisk in flour and heat until bubbly. Gradually add milk, stirring constantly until sauce thickens. Season with salt and pepper. Add diced cheese to white sauce and stir until cheese melts.

Casserole: In a small saucepan, melt 2 tablespoons butter. Add breadcrumbs and stir until thoroughly coated with butter. Set aside. Add steamed, chopped asparagus to the cheese sauce and mix well. Add chopped eggs last and gently mix. Pour mixture into a 2-quart baking dish. Sprinkle bread crumbs over top of mixture. Bake at 375°, uncovered, for 15 minutes or until bread crumbs are nicely browned.

Try broccoli florets in place of asparagus. Swiss cheese may be used in place of Cheddar cheese.

Desserts

Irish Cupcakes, recipe page 176

You are invited to a

PHANTOM
VALENTINE PARTY

to help further the work of the
Women's Board of the Jefferson Hospital
Your acceptance is this card of hearts
with a heartening donation

Make checks payable to
The Women's Board of Jefferson Hospital
and
Send in enclosed envelope to

Mrs. P. B. Bland
135 S. 18th St., Phila. 3, Pa.

Best Ever Lemon Bars

2 DOZEN

Freezes well.

CRUST

1	cup unsalted butter	½	cup sifted confectioners' sugar, plus extra for garnish
2	cups flour, sifted		

FILLING

4	large eggs, room temperature	1	tablespoon flour
2	cups granulated sugar	1	pinch salt
2	large lemons, zested	½	teaspoon baking powder
6	tablespoons lemon juice		

Crust: In a large bowl, beat butter, flour and confectioners' sugar together. Pour mixture into a greased 9x13-inch baking dish and pat into a thin layer on the bottom of dish. Bake in 325° oven for 15 minutes.

Filling: In a mixing bowl, beat eggs and granulated sugar until light. Mix in lemon zest and juice. Add flour, salt and baking powder. Combine well. Pour filling into warm or cool baked crust and return to oven for 40 minutes or until filling is set (top may turn brown before filling is completely set). Loosen crust from edges. Cut into squares when cool and dust with confectioners' sugar.

1773

A spring shad run saved George Washington's army from starvation at Valley Forge.

Sicilian Cannoli

2	cups ricotta cheese	⅓	cup pistachios, unsalted and chopped
2	ounces goat cheese		
¼	cup confectioners' sugar	2	ounces bittersweet chocolate, grated
1	teaspoon orange oil		
	zest of 1 orange		premade cannoli shells
¼	teaspoon cinnamon		

Beat cheeses, sugar, orange oil, zest and cinnamon with electric mixer for 1 minute, being careful not to overbeat. Fold in pistachios and chocolate. Chill for 1 hour and fill shells using a pastry bag. Serve immediately.

Pumpkin Pie Like No Other

6-8 SERVINGS

1	(15 ounce) can pumpkin	½	teaspoon nutmeg
1	(14 ounce) can condensed milk	½	teaspoon salt
1	egg	1	(9 inch) graham cracker pie crust
¾	teaspoon cinnamon		
½	teaspoon ginger		

TOPPING

¼	cup brown sugar	2	tablespoons cold margarine
2	tablespoons flour	¾	cup walnuts, chopped
½	teaspoon cinnamon		

Combine first 7 ingredients, mix well and pour into pie crust. Bake at 425° for 15 minutes. Remove pie from oven and lower temperature to 350°.
Topping: Combine brown sugar, flour and cinnamon. Cut in margarine until crumbly, and then add walnuts. Sprinkle on top of pie. Bake pie for an additional 40 minutes or until knife inserted in center comes out clean.

Chocolate Decadence

8-10 PIECES

This recipe has been graciously donated by Jon Jividen of 12th Street Catering.

1	pound dark semisweet chocolate	1	tablespoon flour
5	ounces unsalted butter	5	eggs
1	tablespoon sugar	1	teaspoon pure vanilla extract

Melt chocolate and butter together in a double boiler. Sift flour and sugar together. Whip eggs with vanilla until thick (consistency should be like a thin cake batter). Fold flour/sugar mixture into egg mixture. Fold in melted chocolate. Pour mixture into a 9 inch greased and floured cake pan. Bake in a 400° oven for approximately 10 minutes or until edge begin to crack. Remove from oven and transfer to refrigerator. Let chill. Remove from pan by heating bottom of the pan slightly. Cut into 8 to 10 pieces. Top with whipped cream, drizzled white chocolate, a dusting of confectioners' sugar or fresh berries if desired.

Buttermilk Yellow Cake

This delicious cake can be served with fresh fruit and whipped cream or frosted with your favorite icing. (See "Simply Incredible Chocolate Icing" in Potpourri Chapter, see page 198).

1	cup butter		3	cups cake flour, sifted
2	cups granulated sugar		½	teaspoon baking soda
4	eggs		1	cup buttermilk

Cream butter and sugar until fluffy. Add eggs, one at a time. Add baking soda to buttermilk. Add flour and buttermilk mixture to the butter, eggs and sugar. Bake in 13x9x2-inch pan at 350° for approximately 30 minutes.

Sour Cream Cookies

3 DOZEN

Batter can be chilled overnight.

½	cup butter, softened		2¾	cups sifted flour
1½	cups sugar		½	teaspoon baking soda
2	eggs		½	teaspoon baking powder
1	cup sour cream		½	teaspoon salt
1	teaspoon vanilla			

Mix butter, sugar and eggs together thoroughly. Stir in sour cream and vanilla. Sift together flour, baking soda, baking powder and salt: stir into sour cream mixture. Chill for at least 1 hour. Drop rounded teaspoons about 2 inches apart on lightly greased baking sheet. Bake at 425° for about 8 to 10 minutes, just until when touched lightly with finger and no imprint remains.

This is a soft cookie.

2002

John and Kira's Chocolates, founded by John Doyle and Kira Baker-Doyle, focuses on creating products that highlight ingredients from small family producers and urban gardens. With Project Mintpatch, the company uses mint grown by Drew Elementary and University City High School students to flavor their chocolates.

The non-sectarian Jefferson Meditation Room (Jefferson Chapel) has been one of the Women's Board longest enduring projects, originally dedicated in 1956. The space was refurbished and re-dedicated in 2011 to honor the contributions of Past President Elaine Abruzzo.

Rocky Road Confection

12 SERVINGS

1 (12 ounce) package semisweet chocolate morsels

1 (14 ounce) can sweetened condensed milk

2 tablespoons margarine or butter

2 cups dry roasted peanuts

1 (10 ounce) package miniature white marshmallows

½ cup raisins

Line a 9x13-inch pan with waxed paper. In top of double boiler, over boiling water, melt morsels with sweetened condensed milk and margarine. Remove from heat. Put nuts and marshmallows in a large bowl, then fold in chocolate mixture and raisins. Spread in a waxed paper lined pan. Chill until firm. Turn pan over and remove from pan. Peel off waxed paper. Cut into desired size. Cover and store at room temperature.

Banana Chocolate Chip Bread

3 LOAVES

Freezes well.

3 eggs, beaten

1 cup vegetable oil

1¾ cups sugar

2 cups chocolate chip morsels

3 cups flour

2 teaspoons vanilla

1 teaspoon salt

1 teaspoon baking soda

½ teaspoon baking powder

3-4 very ripe bananas (brown to black outside; number needed depends on size of bananas)

Beat eggs until fluffy. Add in all other ingredients. Turn into 3 medium-size (9x5-inch) loaf pans, lightly greased. Bake at 325° for 1 hour. Insert toothpick into center, when comes out clean, bread is done.

May substitute peanut butter morsels for chocolate chips.

Mississippi Mud

2 SERVINGS

Dessert with a kick!

1½	ounces Southern Comfort™
1½	ounces coffee flavored liqueur
2	large scoops vanilla ice cream

Semisweet chocolate shavings, for garnish

Place ice cream, Southern Comfort™ and coffee liqueur in a blender and blend until thick. Spoon into cocktail glasses and garnish with shaved chocolate.

Ting-A-Lings

Easy to make and delicious!

12 ounces white chocolate chips
1½ cups chow mein noodles
1 cup salted peanuts

Line cookie sheet with waxed paper. On medium power, microwave white chocolate chips in microwave safe dish for 3 to 4 minutes stirring once halfway through. When chocolate is melted, stir in chow mein noodles and peanuts. Use teaspoon measure and drop mix onto wax paper. Let stand until set. Store in refrigerator.

Van's Cookies

2 DOZEN COOKIES

½ cup butter
1 cup granulated sugar
½ cup vegetable oil
1 egg
1 teaspoon vanilla
2½ cups flour, sifted
½ teaspoon baking powder
¼ teaspoon salt
ground nuts for tops of cookies

Cream butter, sugar and vegetable oil. Beat in egg and vanilla. Add sifted flour, baking soda and salt. Roll to walnut sized balls, and then flatten with glass dipped in sugar. Sprinkle with ground nuts and bake at 350° until light brown (8 to 10 minutes).

1876

Hires root beer was given away free of charge to visitors to the 1876 Centennial Fair. It was marketed as a solid concentrate of 16 wild roots and berries. It claimed to purify the blood and make one's cheeks rosy.

City Tavern, located on Second Street was constructed in the latest architectural style in 1773. It had several large club rooms and a number of commodious lodging rooms.

Snickerdoodle Cake

CAKE

1	package plain white cake mix	2	teaspoons cinnamon
1	cup milk		vegetable shortening or spray for greasing pans
8	tablespoons butter, melted		flour for dusting pans
3	large eggs		
1	teaspoon vanilla extract		

BUTTER CREAM FROSTING

8	tablespoons butter, at room temperature	3-4	tablespoons milk
3¾	cups confectioners' sugar, sifted	2	teaspoons vanilla extract
		½	teaspoon cinnamon

Cake: Place a rack in the center of the oven and preheat to 350°. Grease 2 (9 inch) round cake pans with shortening or spray and flour pans lightly. Mix cake mix, milk, melted butter, eggs, vanilla and cinnamon in a large mixing bowl. Blend together at a low speed for 1 minute, scraping down sides. Beat for about 2 minutes at a medium speed until well mixed. Divide that batter between the two prepared cake rounds. Place pans side by side in oven. Bake for 27 to 29 minutes or until cake springs back when lightly depressed with finger. Place baked rounds on a cooling rack. Let cool for 10 minutes. Loosen cake edges with a knife and invert onto a rack, then invert again so cakes are right side up. Allow to cool for at least 30 minutes. Prepare the Butter Cream Frosting while waiting.

Butter Cream Frosting: Beat butter until fluffy (30 seconds). Add all remaining ingredients. Beat for 1 minute. If too stiff, add the rest of the milk. Place one cake round, right side up, on a cake plate. Frost the top. Place the second layer, right side up, on top of the first round. Frost the sides then top of the layered cake. Use clean, smooth strokes. Sprinkle top with cinnamon through a strainer for an attractive effect.

Pennywise Date and Nut Cookie Bars

8-10 SERVINGS

½ cup butter
1½ cups light brown sugar, divided
1 cup flour
1 cup chopped nuts
3 tablespoons flour

½ teaspoon salt
1 cup dates, chopped
2 eggs, beaten slightly
confectioners' sugar, for dusting

Mix butter, ½ cup brown sugar and flour. Press into 8x8-inch pan and bake for 10 to 12 minutes in a 350° oven, pricking with a fork before baking. Mix remaining 1 cup brown sugar, nuts, flour, salt, dates and eggs; spread on top. Return to oven and bake 20 to 22 minutes at 350°. Cut when cool and dust with confectioners' sugar.

Pumpkin Cake and Cream Cheese Icing

Great for the holiday season!

CAKE

2 cups flour
2 tablespoons baking soda
2 teaspoons cinnamon
1 teaspoon baking powder

2 cups sugar
1 cup oil
4 eggs
1 pound canned pumpkin

CREAM CHEESE ICING

1 stick butter
8 ounces cream cheese

1 (1 pound) box confectioners' sugar
2 teaspoons vanilla

Cake: Mix dry ingredients in one bowl and wet ingredients in another. Gradually combine the two and bake in a greased tube pan. Bake for 1 hour at 350° or until inserted toothpick comes out clean. Icing: Prepare icing by creaming butter, cream cheese, confectioners' sugar and vanilla together. Ice cake when it has cooled.

2012

Philadelphia's Éclat Chocolates was named the "Best Chocolates in America" by Bon Appetit magazine.

Pecan Pie

6-8 SERVINGS

If real barrel molasses is not available, use dark Karo syrup.

1	cup sugar	½	cup butter
½	teaspoon salt	1½	teaspoons vanilla
1	cup molasses	2	cups pecans
3	eggs, beaten	1	(9 inch) pie crust

Simmer sugar, salt and molasses until sugar melts. Add butter, vanilla and pecans. Add eggs. Place mixture into pie crust and bake for 40 minutes at 350°.

Raspberry Jam Crumb Cake

8-10 SERVINGS

This cake freezes very well.

CRUMB TOPPING

6	tablespoons unsalted butter, melted	¾	teaspoon cinnamon
¼	cup brown sugar, packed	⅛	teaspoon salt
¼	cup sugar	1	cup and 2 tablespoons flour

CAKE

1	cup flour	½	cup milk
½	cup sugar	1	large egg
1¾	teaspoons baking powder	1	teaspoon vanilla
6	tablespoons butter, melted	⅓	cup seedless raspberry jam

Preheat oven to 400°. Butter and flour a 9 inch square baking pan.

Crumb Topping: Make topping by whisking together melted butter, sugars, cinnamon and salt until smooth. Stir in flour and combine with fork until crumbs form. Set aside.

Cake: Make cake by whisking together flour, sugar, baking powder and salt. In a larger bowl, whisk butter, milk, egg and vanilla. Whisk in the flour mixture until just combined. Pour batter into prepared pan. Place a dollop of jam over top and swirl with knife. Cover evenly with crumb mixture and bake for 25 to 30 minutes until wooden toothpick comes out clean. Cool on rack for 10 to 15 minutes.

Healthy Oatmeal Cookies

MAKES 3 DOZEN COOKIES

Only 68 calories per cookie!

2	cups quick oats	2	egg whites, beaten until fluffy
1	cup brown sugar, packed	¼	teaspoon salt
½	cup olive oil	½	teaspoon almond extract

Stir together oats, sugar and olive oil. Beat egg whites into mixture. Stir in salt and almond extract. Drop by teaspoon onto a lightly oiled baking sheet. Bake in a 325° oven for 15 minutes. Cool for 10 minutes before removing.

Chocolate Crunch Bars

32 SQUARES

Perfect for a crowd and can be made the day before.

4	tablespoons butter, softened	3	tablespoons cocoa powder
¼	cup canola oil	1	(10½ ounce) bag miniature marshmallows
1½	cups sugar		
3	eggs	1	(12 ounce) bag semisweet chocolate chips
1	teaspoon vanilla		
1⅓	cups white flour	1	cup natural peanut butter
½	teaspoon baking powder	2	cups crisp rice cereal
½	teaspoon salt		

Preheat oven to 350°. In a large bowl, cream butter with oil and add sugar. Beat eggs in, one at a time, adding vanilla and beating until fluffy. In a medium bowl, combine flour, baking powder, salt and cocoa. Add flour mixture to wet ingredients and combine well. Spread in an 11½x16½-inch jelly-roll pan and bake for 15 minutes. Remove and sprinkle marshmallows evenly over cake and return to oven for 2 minutes. Remove and, working quickly, spread melted marshmallows over cake. While cake is baking, in a medium saucepan melt chocolate chips and peanut butter over low heat. Stir mixture to combine well. Remove from heat and stir in rice cereal. Allow cake to cool and chill before cutting.

1866

Breyer's Ice Cream is founded by William Breyer in his Philadelphia kitchen. He sold the ice cream to people in the neighborhood out of a horse-drawn wagon. The wagon was pulled by his white horse named Peacock.

Sir William Osler, observed, "The trained nurse has become one of the great blessings to humanity, taking a place beside the physician and the priest, and not inferior to either in her mission."

Irish Cupcakes *(pictured)*

24 CUPCAKES

CUPCAKES

1	cup stout (a dark beer)	2	cups granulated sugar
1	cup salted butter, softened to room temperature	1½	teaspoons baking soda
¾	cup cocoa powder	½	teaspoon salt
2	cups all-purpose flour	2	eggs
		⅔	cup sour cream

GANACHE FILLING

8	ounces semisweet chocolate chunks	2	tablespoons salted butter, softened to room temperature
⅔	cup heavy cream	5	tablespoons Irish whiskey

FROSTING

2	cups salted butter, softened to room temperature	5	cups confectioners' sugar
		12	tablespoons Irish cream liqueur

Cupcakes: Preheat oven to 350°. Line 24 cupcake tins with liners. Bring the stout and butter to a simmer in a medium saucepan over medium heat. Add cocoa powder and whisk until mixture is smooth. Cool slightly. Whisk flour, sugar, baking soda and salt in large bowl to combine. Using an electric mixture, beat eggs and sour cream on medium speed until combined. Add the stout mixture to the egg mixture and beat until just combined. Reduce speed to low, add the flour mixture and beat briefly until completely combined. Divide the batter among the cupcake liners. Bake until a toothpick inserted into the center comes out clean (about 17 minutes). Cool the cupcakes.

Ganache Filling: Finely chop the chocolate chunks and transfer to a heatproof bowl. Heat the cream until simmering and pour it over the chocolate. Let it sit for 1 minute and then, using a rubber spatula, stir it from the center outward until smooth. Add butter and whiskey and stir until combined. Add more whiskey to taste, if necessary. Let ganache cool until thick but soft enough to be piped.

Fill the cupcakes by cutting out a cubic inch of the center of cooled cupcakes, going about ⅔ of the way down. Transfer ganache to a piping back with a wide tip and fill holes in each cupcake to the top. (Recipe continued on next page.)

Frosting: Whip butter on medium speed for 5 minutes, scraping the sides of the bowl occasionally. Reduce speed to medium low and gradually add the confectioners' sugar until all of it is incorporated. Add Irish cream, increasing the speed to medium high and whip for another 2 to 3 minutes, until it is light and fluffy. Add more Irish cream liqueur to taste.

Bride's Pudding

According to legend, the daughter of a baker did not like cake, so instead he prepared this pudding for his daughter's wedding. Enjoy this beautiful and finger-licking good dessert!

2	envelopes unflavored gelatin	¾	cup sugar
1	cup water	2	cups heavy cream, whipped
6	egg whites	1	teaspoon vanilla extract
¼	teaspoon salt	3½	ounce can coconut, shredded

Prepare the pan before beginning recipe by buttering a round 9x3-inch springform pan well and pressing 3 tablespoons coconut into sides and bottom of pan. Set pan aside. Next, with either electric or hand mixer, beat heavy cream until thick and fluffy. Refrigerate. Soften gelatin in a small bowl with ½ cup cold water and then add ½ cup boiling water and stir to thoroughly dissolve gelatin. Cool for 15 minutes. In a separate bowl, beat egg whites with salt until frothy. Gradually beat in sugar, continue beating until peaks form when beaters are lifted. Gradually beat in cooled gelatin and gently fold in whipped cream and vanilla. Pour into prepared springform pan. Chill until firm. Remove from springform pan. Garnish with sugared violets and remaining coconut before serving.

1914

Tasty Baking Company, maker of Tastykake foods, was established in 1914 by Philip J. Baur and Herbert T. Morris. Gross sales at the end of that year were $300,000. They were the first company to sell individually packaged cakes.

1859

The Civil War brought much change to the Jefferson Medical College, as a large portion of the medical class was comprised of students from the South. There was a massive exodus of 200 Southern students from Jefferson and the University of Pennsylvania during the war. Enrollment had re-stabilized by 1865.

Jinx's Apple Cake

6	Granny Smith apples	½	cup orange juice
5	teaspoons cinnamon	1	cup vegetable oil
2½	cups white sugar, divided	2½	teaspoons vanilla extract
1	cup golden raisins	3	cups flour
1½	cups chopped walnuts	3	teaspoons baking powder
4	eggs		

Preheat oven to 350°. Peel, core apples and cut into chunks. Combine apples, cinnamon and ½ cup sugar. Plump raisins in hot water. Let sit 10 minutes, drain. Add raisins and walnuts to apple mixture. Set aside. Beat eggs lightly. Add orange juice, oil and vanilla. Mix well. Combine remaining 2 cups of sugar, flour, and baking powder and slowly pour in liquids. In a heavily greased tube pan place one-half the batter, then half of the apple mixture, then the rest of the batter, and the remaining apples. Cover with foil. Bake 1 hour, uncover. Bake an additional 40 minutes to 1 hour, until an inserted toothpick comes out clean.

Blueberry Crisp

8 SERVINGS

Delicious when served with a scoop of vanilla ice cream!

2½	cups fresh blueberries	⅓	cup unsalted butter, melted
⅔	cup brown sugar, packed	¾	teaspoon ground cinnamon
½	cup all-purpose flour	¾	teaspoon ground nutmeg
¾	cup quick cooking or old-fashioned oats		

Rinse and drain blueberries and place in the bottom of a 2 quart, greased glass baking dish. Mix brown sugar, flour, oats, butter, cinnamon and nutmeg with a fork. (Mixture will be crumbly.) Sprinkle and mix evenly over blueberries. Bake at 350° for 30 minutes or until topping is golden brown and blueberries are tender when pierced with a fork. Serve warm.

Traditional Butterscotch Pudding

- ½ cup packed dark brown sugar
- 2 tablespoons plus 2 teaspoons cornstarch
- ¼ teaspoon salt
- 1½ cups whole milk
- ½ cup heavy cream
- 2 tablespoons unsalted butter, cut into bits
- 1 teaspoon pure vanilla extract
- whipped cream

Whisk together brown sugar, cornstarch and ¼ teaspoon salt in a heavy medium saucepan, then whisk in milk and cream. Bring to a boil over medium heat, whisking frequently. Allow to boil while whisking for 1 minute. Remove from heat and whisk in butter and vanilla. Pour into a medium size bowl or individual serving bowls. Cover with buttered waxed paper and chill until cold—at least 1½ hours. Garnish with whipped cream, beaten until fluffy and sweetened with a bit of sugar.

May serve warm if preferred.

Toffee and Chocolate Bar Cookies

Easy to make and freezes beautifully!

- 8 tablespoons butter
- 1 cup brown sugar
- 1 sleeve club crackers
- 12 ounces chocolate chips
- ½ cup chopped walnuts

Arrange crackers side by side on cookie sheet. Melt butter and sugar in a small pan over medium high heat. Heat for 5 minutes stirring often. Bake crackers at 350° for 5 minutes. Pour sugar and butter over crackers. Immediately sprinkle chocolate chips over top and spread as they melt over crackers. Sprinkle with nuts. Refrigerate for at least 2 hours. Break apart into different sized pieces and serve.

1984

Rita's Water Ice, a popular warm weather treat, was founded by former Philadelphia firefighter, Bob Tumelo.

George McClellan, MD, grandson of the founder of the Jefferson Medical College, was also a Jefferson graduate. He went on to write two important anatomy textbooks of his day.

Philadelphia Pretzel Pie

Fun to make with children!

CRUST

1¼	cups hard pretzels (your choice of type)	¼	cup softened butter or margarine
¼	cup sugar		

FILLING

1-1½	quarts vanilla ice cream, softened	⅓	cup coarsely chopped pretzels

Crust: In a blender, crush pretzels. In a mixing bowl, combine pretzel crumbs, sugar and butter; mix until well blended. Press into a 9-inch pie pan to form a crust. Bake at 375° for 6 to 8 minutes. Cool.

Filling: Fill the prepared crust with softened ice cream and pretzel mix; freeze. Garnish with peanuts, chocolate sauce or fruit.

Vary type of pretzels and ice cream flavors! May use gluten free pretzels.

The Original Shortbread Cookie Recipe

The Barton Committee's Shortbread Cookies were the Highlight of the Old Market Fair Baked Goods Booth. Don't Try This at Home!!

90	pounds butter	1	cup salt
3	cups vanilla extract	120	pounds flour
60	pounds superfine sugar	1	cup baking soda

Mix dough thoroughly and divide into 15# portions. Spread dough onto cookie sheets, aerate, and place wooden frame over cookie sheet. Bake at 325° for 50 to 55 minutes.

The Barton Committee's Famous Shortbread Cookies
(As told by Mrs. Audrey Knowles)

1968-1974

The original shortbread recipe was obtained in Hawaii by Mrs. Josephine Dustin, while on holiday. The shortbreads were made as a fund raiser and sold throughout the Island. Mr. Clarence Dustin fashioned the cutting and aerator systems. Dr. Harry Knowles made the wooden frames that were placed over the dough on the cookie sheets. It would typically take 15-20 Barton Committee members, and often their spouses, to make the shortbread cookies. Mrs. Schaeffer, the Honorary Cookie Chairman, Sally Luscombe, Marge Connolly, Marge Davis, Carolyn Freidman, Margaret Herbut, Marie McCloskey, Barbara Marks, Sally Ramsey, Ann Baldridge and her husband, the Dean of the School of Allied Health, Ruby Sokoloff, Jean Wagner, and Audrey Knowles all participated.

Beginning at 7 A.M. on a Sunday in the Jefferson Hospital cafeteria the cookies would be baked. It would take all day to make 6 batches of cookies - a batch contained about 400 cookies! The shortbreads were sold annually at the Emergency Aid Christmas Bazaar and at the Jefferson Old Market Fair in a bag of 24 pieces for $1.00 initially. Later when the price of butter rose, 18 pieces sold for $2.00! The Barton Committee made the cookies for 6 years, until the price of the ingredients reduced profitability. These cookies remain legendary in the halls of the Thomas Jefferson University Hospital.

2005

The Jefferson School of Nursing attained university status in 2005. Dr. Mary Schaal, EdD, RN (Class of 1963) was selected as the Inaugural Dean and guided the School until 2011.

Spiced Pumpkin Cheesecake

You will need a 9-inch round springform pan for this recipe.

CRUST

38 gingersnaps, finely crushed	¼ cup butter, melted
¼ cup finely chopped pecans, packed tightly	

CHEESECAKE

4 (8 ounce) packages Philadelphia™ Cream Cheese, softened	1 (15 ounce) can pumpkin
	1 tablespoon lemon juice
	1 teaspoon vanilla extract
1 cup sugar	4 eggs

TOPPING

1 cup heavy whipped cream	½ teaspoon cinnamon
1-2 tablespoons sugar	

Crust: Mix gingersnap crumbs, nuts and melted butter together. Press onto bottom and sides of a 9-inch springform pan.

Cheesecake: Beat cream cheese and sugar with a hand mixer until well blended. Add pumpkin, lemon juice and vanilla. Mix well. Add eggs, one at a time, mixing well after each egg. Pour mixture into the crust and bake at 325° for 1 hour and 15 to 30 minutes, or until center is almost solid. Loosen cake from rim of pan. Cool completely before removing cake from pan. Refrigerate for at least 4 hours.

Topping: Pour heavy whipping cream in a deep bowl and add 1 to 2 tablespoons sugar. Beat with a mixer until forms soft peaks. Serve topped with whipped heavy cream and a dusting of cinnamon.

Banana Pudding

Best made a day ahead to allow flavors to blend.

BANANAS

5   very ripe medium bananas

CUSTARD

2 cups milk	1 tablespoon butter
⅔ cup sugar, divided	2 tablespoons vanilla extract
2 tablespoons cornstarch	12 ounces frozen fat-free whipped topping
¼ teaspoon salt	
2 large eggs	45 vanilla wafers

Bananas: Place bananas on a jelly-roll pan covered with parchment paper or silicone baking sheet. Bake bananas at 350° for 20 minutes. Cool completely 3 of the bananas, peel and cut into ½-inch slices. Set aside. Bake other 2 bananas for an additional 20 minutes. Cool last 2 bananas and carefully peel and place in a small bowl. Mash with a fork until a smooth consistency.

Custard: Combine milk and ⅓ cup sugar in a saucepan over medium heat. Simmer, but do not bring to a boil. Combine remaining sugar, cornstarch, salt and eggs in a mixing bowl. Stir with a whisk. Gradually add hot mixture to this, whisking constantly. Return mixture to saucepan and cook over medium heat until thick and bubbly. Add mashed bananas, butter and vanilla; stir until butter melts. Place saucepan in a large ice-filled bowl for 15 minutes, stir occasionally. Fold half of whipped topping into pudding.

Spread 1 cup of the custard over the bottom of an 11x7-inch baking pan. Top with 20 vanilla wafers and half of the banana slices. Spoon half of remaining custard over bananas. Top with 20 vanilla wafers and banana slices and custard. Spread remaining whipped topping over top. Crush remaining 5 vanilla wafers and sprinkle over top. Refrigerate for a least 1 hour before serving.

1885

Lewis Dubois Bassett, a Quaker school teacher and farmer, began selling his ice cream from a location at 5th & Market Streets in Philadelphia.

Jefferson Medical College boasts the largest medical alumni of all U.S. medical schools with more than 30,000 members.

Rudy's Olde Fashioned Rice Pudding

4	eggs, beaten
3	cups milk or half-and-half (or use ½ milk and ½ half-and-half)
⅓	cup sugar
½	teaspoon salt
2	teaspoons vanilla extract
2	cups cooked white or brown rice
½	cup raisins
	cinnamon for sprinkling

Mix all ingredients together except cinnamon. Pour into a 2½ quart baking dish. Set dish in a pan of hot water. Bake at 350° for 30 minutes. Then stir from bottom of pan. Return to oven and bake until knife inserted in middle of dish comes out clean. Sprinkle cinnamon over top of pudding when it is done baking. Serve hot with a drop of milk or half-and-half.

Grasshopper Brownies

1	box fudge brownie mix (21 to 23 ounces) or your own recipe

TOPPING

1	pound confectioners' sugar	7	tablespoons butter, melted
	dash salt	1½	teaspoons mint extract
5	tablespoons milk	1-2	drops green food coloring

GLAZE

1½	tablespoons butter	2	squares unsweetened baking chocolate

Grease a 13x9x2-inch oblong pan. Mix brownies—may add ½ cup chopped pecans or walnuts if desired. Bake as directed. Cool brownies.
Topping: Mix topping ingredients until smooth and spread on cooled brownies. Refrigerate for at least 1 hour.
Glaze: Melt butter and chocolate. Pour over mint frosting. Tilt pan back and forth until fully glazed. Refrigerate until ready to serve.

Fun to serve on St. Patrick's Day!

Oreo™ Cheesecake

Keeps for 3 days in refrigerator.

CRUST

25	crushed Oreo™ cookies (makes 2½ cups crumbs)	4	tablespoons melted butter

FILLING

4	packages Philadelphia Cream Cheese™	4	large eggs, at room temperature
1¼	cups sugar plus ¼ cup sugar	3	large egg yolks
2	tablespoons flour	2	cups sour cream
1¾	cups chopped Oreos	⅓	cup whipping cream
		1	tablespoon vanilla extract

Preheat oven to 425°.

Crust: Combine Oreo™ crumbs and melted butter and mix well. Butter a large springform pan (10½x2 or 9x3-inch). Pat crust mixture into pan on bottom and ⅔ way up the sides. Refrigerate until filling is ready.

Filling: Beat cream cheese until smooth, add 1¼ cups sugar and beat until light, about 3 minutes. While beating, add eggs and egg yolks, then beat in whipping cream, flour and 1 tablespoon vanilla. Pour ½ batter onto crust, sprinkle chopped Oreos™ over batter, then cover with remaining batter. Put pan on a cookie sheet and bake at 425° for 15 minutes. Reduce oven temperature to 225° and bake for 50 minutes or until cake is set. Remove cake from oven and increase oven temperature to 350°. Stir together remaining ¼ cup sugar, 1 teaspoon vanilla and 2 cups sour cream. Spread on top of cake and bake for 7 minutes.

Cool in a draft-free area until cake is room temperature. Refrigerate for at least 3 hours before serving. Serve chilled.

Garnish with an Oreo™ cookie on top.

Frozen Macaroon Sherbet Treat

A refreshing summer dessert!

1	pint heavy whipping cream	1	pint raspberry sherbet
1	teaspoon sugar	1	pint lemon sherbet
16	coconut macaroon cookies	1	pint strawberry sherbet
1	cup chopped walnuts		fresh mint leaves

Whip cream with sugar until thickened. Crumble macaroons in a bowl and add walnuts. Mix whipped cream and macaroons together. Spread ½ of the mixture in a 9x13-inch pan. Then create a colorful layer by spreading alternating scoops of the sherbets over the whipped cream-macaroon layer. Spread remaining whipped cream-macaroon mixture over sherbet layer. Freeze well. Allow dessert to soften for 10 minutes before serving. Serve with a mint leaf.

Rhubarb Jewel Cake
1 CAKE

CAKE

2	eggs	2	cups flour
1¼	cups sugar	3½	cups fresh cubed rhubarb
1	teaspoon baking soda	1	cup sour cream
½	teaspoon salt		

TOPPING

1	cup sugar	¼	cup flour
¼	cup butter or margarine		

Cake: Mix all cake ingredients together using a mixer. Pour into a 9x13-inch baking pan greased with cooking spray.

Topping: Combine topping ingredients and mix until crumbly. Sprinkle over cake batter. Bake at 350° for 45 minutes. Cool before serving.

Potpourri

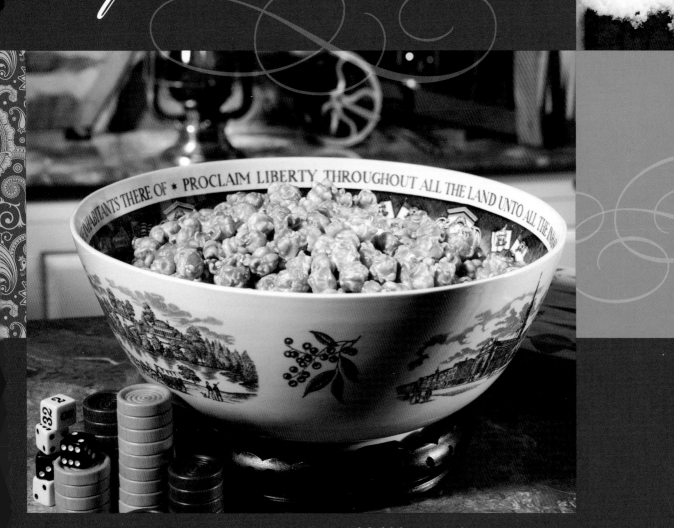

Philadelphia Caramel Corn, recipe page 189

Jefferson Jewel

The Thirtieth Annual

Jefferson
Jewel

Presented by The Women's Board of
Thomas Jefferson University Hospital

Cocktails, Light Fare, Jazz Trio
and the Jefferson Jewel Drawing

Sunday, September 14, 2003
Four to six o'clock

At Ardrossan
The Family Home of
Robert Montgomery Scott
Newtown Road
Villanova, Pennsylvania

Philadelphia Caramel Corn *(pictured)* — 8 QUARTS

2	cups light brown sugar		1	teaspoon salt
½	cup light corn syrup		1	teaspoon baking soda
½	pound butter		8	quarts popped microwave popcorn
¼	teaspoon cream of tartar			

Combine brown sugar, corn syrup, butter, cream of tartar and salt in a 3-quart saucepan and bring to a boil over medium heat. Stir constantly until it reaches 250° or at a hard-ball stage, add baking soda. Pour over popped corn in a large roasting pan. Stir to coat popped corn. Bake at 200° for 1 hour, stirring occasionally. Spread on waxed paper to cool.

Air Fare — 2 SANDWICHES

Great to bring along for lunch or dinner on a trip!

1	fresh baguette, small		12	basil leaves
4	tablespoons olive oil		¼	English cucumber, thinly sliced
1	teaspoon red wine vinegar		¼	cup chopped olives, any kind
1	clove garlic			salt and pepper
½	small red onion		3	ounces mozzarella cheese, sliced
1	medium tomato, thinly sliced			

Cut baguette lengthwise. Combine oil, vinegar and garlic in a bowl and whisk to emulsify. Add onion, tomato, basil, cucumber, chopped olives and salt and pepper. Toss and allow to marinate for 15 to 20 minutes. On one side of the baguette, place tomatoes, onions, cucumbers and mozzarella. Spoon the remaining ingredients and liquid on top. Top with remaining side of baguette. Cut in half. Wrap tightly in cling wrap and then foil. Refrigerate until ready for trip. Sandwich should be soggy — the longer the baguette absorbs the filling, the better!

1876

Animal Crackers were introduced by Walter G. Wilson from his shop at 212/214 North Front Street for the Centennial Exposition.

Ricotta and Fig Sandwich with Truffle Oil

1 SERVING

This sandwich is very rich and probably better split between two people.

2	slices multigrain bread		handful arugula
¼	cup ricotta cheese		drizzle of truffle oil
3	tablespoons fig jam		pinch of sea salt

Toast the bread. Spread fig jam on both sides. Layer ricotta on one side. Flavor ricotta with sea salt. On the other slice put the arugula. Drizzle ricotta and arugula with truffle oil. Close sandwich. Cut and serve.

Homemade Marinara Sauce

6 SERVINGS

High quality canned tomatoes will make a big difference in this sauce!

3	tablespoons olive oil	3-4	fresh basil leaves, coarsely chopped
½	medium sized onion, minced		salt and pepper to taste
½	teaspoon salt	3	ounces grated Parmesan cheese (optional)
3	cloves garlic, minced		
2	large cans plum tomatoes		
1	teaspoon sugar		

Heat olive oil in medium saucepan over medium heat. Add minced onion and ½ teaspoon salt and sauté until golden (about 5 minutes). Add minced garlic and cook until fragrant (about 30 seconds). Put tomatoes in blender or chop with knife. Add tomatoes and sugar to the pan. Increase heat to high and bring to simmer. Lower heat to medium-low and bring to simmer. Cook for 30 minutes. Remove from heat and add basil and salt and pepper to taste. Top with grated Parmesan cheese.

Irish Potatoes

No cooking involved in this St. Patrick's Day treat ... fun for the kids to make!

½	cup softened butter	16	ounces confectioners' sugar
¼	teaspoon salt	3½	ounces flaked coconut
1	teaspoon vanilla extract		ground cinnamon

Combine butter, salt, vanilla, sugar and coconut. Mix with hands. Shape into balls about ½-inch in diameter. Roll balls in cinnamon to coat. Eat!

Pumpkin Apple Dip

2 CUPS

Great as an after school snack and easy for children to make themselves!

8	ounces cream cheese, softened	2	tablespoons maple syrup
½	cup brown sugar	1	teaspoon cinnamon
½	cup canned pumpkin		apple slices

Beat brown sugar and cream cheese until smooth. Mix in pumpkin, maple syrup and cinnamon. Delicious served with apple slices or gingersnap cookies.

This can be made with fat free cream cheese.

Brie and Nutella Baguettes

"Adult Smores"

1	wheel of Brie cheese	1	baguette loaf
1	jar Nutella		

Slice baguette in half and then down the middle vertically. Spread Nutella on both sides of baguette. Layer slices of Brie on bread. In a 300° preheated oven, roast sandwiches until bread is warm and Brie begins to melt. Watch closely as this can happen quickly! Cut and serve warm.

1818

The first nationally recognized name in ice cream was Parkinson's which was founded by George and Eleanor Parkinson in 1818 at their confectionary shop next to the Pennsylvania Arms Tavern at 180 Chestnut Street. Son James continued the family tradition, culminating in a thousand dollar dinner in 1851 which defeated New York's Delmonico in a cooking challenge.

1992

The Hoagie is declared
the official sandwich
of Philadelphia.

Mini Grilled Cheese Sandwiches

MAKES 4 SANDWICHES

8	slices cocktail size rye bread
16	slices sharp Cheddar cheese
3	tablespoons unsalted butter, softened

Cut cheese to size of cocktail bread. Spread butter on one side of each of 2 slices of bread. Heat a non-stick skillet over medium-high heat. Place buttered side of bread face down in skillet and top with 2 slices of cheese. Top with another slice of bread; butter side up. Cook for 2 minutes, flip sandwich and cook other side for 2 minutes. Cheese should be melted and the bread should be golden brown. (Repeat process for additional sandwiches.) Serve immediately garnished with a dill pickle spear and a side of ketchup or Dijon mustard.

Serve with our Tomato Basil Soup (see page 39)!

Chicken Peanut Pitas

2 SERVINGS

1	cup shredded rotisserie chicken	1	whole-wheat pita pocket, cut in half
⅓	cup green onions, sliced	½	cup bean sprouts
2	tablespoons red bell pepper, sliced thinly	3	tablespoons carrots, cut diagonally
2	tablespoons peanut satay sauce	2	tablespoons fresh cilantro, chopped
⅛	teaspoon kosher salt		

Combine chicken, onions, peppers, satay sauce and salt. Toss to coat evenly. Fill each pita half with chicken mixture, bean sprouts, carrots and cilantro. Serve with Terra Chips™.

May substitute chopped lettuce for bean sprouts.

Raspberry-Orange Lemonade   MAKES 8 CUPS

Serve over ice with a sprig of fresh orange-mint or spearmint on the side or orange slices.

SYRUP

¾   cup sugar

1   cup water

LEMONADE

2   cups fresh raspberries

1   cup water

½   cup juice of freshly squeezed orange

juice of 14 fresh lemons (1¾ cups)

16   ounces sparkling water

orange-mint or spearmint sprigs

Syrup: In a small pot, bring sugar and 1 cup water to a boil. Cook for 2 to 2½ minutes, stirring to dissolve sugar. Cool syrup.

Lemonade: Blend raspberries and 1 cup of water in a blender. Pulse until well blended. Over a large pitcher, pour raspberry mixture through a fine strain to remove seeds. To the pitcher add orange juice, lemon juice, cooled syrup and chilled sparkling water. Serve over ice with a sprig of fresh orange-mint or spearmint sprigs on the side or orange slices.

In place of sparkling water, try substituting champagne, spumanti or prosecco.

Barbecued Chicken Pizza

A kid-friendly pizza pie.

8 ounces pre-made thin pizza crust	½ cup yellow or orange bell pepper, chopped irregularly
⅓ cup barbecue sauce	2-3 plum tomatoes, sliced in thin horizontal pieces
1⅓ cups shredded chicken breast	2 ounces shredded mozzarella cheese
⅓ cup red onion, sliced vertically	

Preheat oven to 500°. Place pizza shell on a baking sheet. Spread barbecue sauce on crust; leave a ½ inch border around crust. Cover with chicken, onions, peppers, and tomatoes, arranged randomly. Sprinkle mozzarella cheese over top. Bake in preheated oven for 10 minutes or until cheese is melted. Crust should be crisp.

Substitute bleu cheese (2 ounces) when making for adults!

Tarragon-Turkey Salad Sandwiches

3 tablespoons canola mayonnaise	¼ cup minced sweet onion
3 tablespoons plain Greek yogurt	4 red leaf lettuce leaves
1 tablespoon fresh lemon juice	4 slices rye sandwich bread
⅛ teaspoon kosher salt	1 tablespoon fresh tarragon (or rosemary), finely chopped
2 cups cooked turkey breast, chopped	

Combine canola mayonnaise, yogurt, lemon juice and salt in a large bowl. Mix in turkey and onion. Top bread with piece of red lettuce leaf and turkey salad. Sprinkle with chopped tarragon or rosemary. Served as open-face sandwich, cut on the diagonal. Garnish with apple slices or sliced dill pickles.

Elegant Cheese Soufflé

1 SOUFFLÉ

4   slices white bread, butter one side and cube
½   pound sharp Cheddar cheese, grated
¾   cup milk
3   eggs, beat with a fork
⅛   teaspoon dry mustard
    salt and pepper to taste

Place bread cubes on bottom of a 2-quart casserole dish. Sprinkle grated cheese evenly over bread. Mix together milk, eggs, mustard and salt and pepper. Pour over bread cheese. Refrigerate at least 1 hour before baking. Bake at 325° for 1 hour and 15 minutes.

Green Tomato Chutney

4 (1 POUND) CANNING JARS

Chutneys improve in flavor if kept for at least several weeks before using.

2   pounds green tomatoes, chopped
1   large onion, chopped
1   pound Granny Smith apples, peeled and chopped
8   ounces sultanas, chopped
8   ounces brown sugar
1   pint malt vinegar
2   tablespoons mustard seeds
1   inch fresh ginger, peeled and finely chopped (may use 2 teaspoons ground ginger)
2   teaspoons cinnamon

Put all ingredients in an 8-quart pot and bring to boil. Simmer uncovered until reduced to a thick mixture. (It should simmer for 2¾ to 3 hours.) Stir occasionally to keep from sticking to pot. Test by scraping a wooden spoon across the bottom of the pan. When the pan bottom appears clear for a while before the chutney slowly fills in the gap, it is ready. There should be very little liquid left.

Put into hot sterilized jars and seal. Label jars when cool.

May use raisins, dried cranberries or chopped dried apricots in place of sultanas. Serve with pork, lamb or chicken.

2011

Robert L. Brent, MD, PhD, a distinguished Professor of pediatric radiology and pathology at Jefferson and at Nemours/A.I. duPont Hospital for Children since 1955, has established four endowed scholarships at Jefferson in his career. In 2011, Dr. Brent and his wife initiated the Robert and Lillian Brent Alumni Giving Incentive Fund to increase alumni giving and inspire generosity in future graduates. Dr. Brent was named the 2011 Castle-Connolly National Physician of the Year in recognition of excellence in clinical care and also was the recipient of the William Liley Medal, which is awarded to pioneers in perinatal medicine.

Potpourri

Homemade Pesto Sauce

2½ CUPS (ENOUGH FOR 8 SERVINGS OF PASTA)

2	garlic cloves, peeled and halved	½	cup olive oil
2	cups fresh basil leaves, densely packed	3	tablespoons butter, softened
		½	cup grated Parmesan cheese
2	tablespoons pine nuts	2	tablespoons Romano cheese

Combine garlic, basil, pine nuts and olive oil in a food processor. By hand, stir in softened butter and cheeses.

Freeze in ice cubes trays for use in the winter.

Béarnaise Sauce

This cannot be reheated because the eggs may scramble, but to serve leftover, refrigerate and take out ahead of time to serve at room temperature.

¼	cup white wine		salt, to taste
¼	cup wine vinegar, red or white	3	egg yolks
1	tablespoon tarragon, dried	½	cup butter, melted
1	tablespoon shallots, chopped		

Put white wine, vinegar, tarragon, shallots and salt in saucepan and cook down to 2 tablespoons. Put in a blender with egg yolks and blend briefly. Slowly drizzle in butter. Serve immediately.

Cran-Raspberry Sauce

Chill for at least 1 hour to allow flavors to blend.

3   (12 ounce) jars seedless red
    raspberry jam

3   (12 ounce) bags cranberries,
    rinsed and patted dry

1½ teaspoons ground cinnamon

¾   teaspoon ground allspice

3   teaspoons lemon zest

Heat jam in large saucepan over medium heat. Add cranberries, cinnamon and allspice. Reduce heat to medium low and cook until cranberries pop, about 8 minutes. Remove from heat and stir in lemon zest.

This recipe can be made gluten-free by using brands of jam and spices that are gluten free.

Versatile Marinade

Don't omit the marjoram; it really makes this marinade.

2   tablespoons vinegar
    (lemon or lime juice for fish)

2   tablespoons olive oil

2   tablespoons rum

2   tablespoons salt

1½ teaspoons sugar (omit for fish)

1   small onion, chopped

1   clove garlic, minced

1   teaspoon black pepper

1   teaspoon marjoram, ground or
    flakes

(1 teaspoon thyme for fish only)

Mix all ingredients together using a whisk. Marinate meat or poultry for 1 hour. (For fish, marinate for 10 minutes.)

To make the marinade as a sauce, add 1 tablespoon flour and 1 tablespoon butter. Heat and stir until thickened.

Grace and Osler later became re-acquainted in Maine and quietly married. When Osler became Sir William Osler, 1st Baronet, Grace took the title of Lady Revere Osler. Her legacy endowed The Lady Grace Revere Osler Professorship of Surgery at Jefferson Medical College Hospital which is commemorated annually with an invited lectureship and program.

Potpourri

While accounts vary, one source claims the first American pretzel was baked in 1861, about 75 miles west of Philadelphia in Lititz, Pennsylvania.

Green Pea and Mint Pesto

Serve with bread and slices of prosciutto – presents beautifully!

10	ounces frozen green peas, defrosted	1	teaspoon sea salt
4	garlic cloves	1	teaspoon black pepper
½	cup grated Parmesan cheese	⅓	cup olive oil
		½	cup mint leaves, packed

Put all ingredients into a food processor and blend. More salt and/or olive oil may be added based on taste.

Simply Incredible Chocolate Icing

ICING FOR A TWO LAYER CAKE

½	bag semisweet chocolate morsels	8	ounces light sour cream

Melt chocolate morsels in a medium saucepan. Stir constantly to prevent chocolate from burning. Remove from heat. Allow chocolate to cool for 3 minutes. Stir in sour cream.

Heavenly Hot Fudge Sauce

3 CUPS

1	cup chocolate chips	1½	cups evaporated milk
½	cup butter	1	teaspoon vanilla extract
2	cups confectioners' sugar		

Melt chocolate chips and butter together. Add sugar and milk. Stir constantly; bring to boil and cook for 8 minutes. Add vanilla and stir.

Fantastic served over vanilla ice cream or on a chocolate cake.

Tangy Barbecue Sauce

Different types of chutney will create different flavors.

12	ounces chili sauce		8	ounces chutney (mango or other)
14	ounces ketchup			
11	ounces A-1 Steak Sauce™		12	drops Tabasco™ sauce
10	ounces Worcestershire sauce			

Combine all ingredients and heat until comes to a boil.

Serve cold on side with sandwiches or to baste ribs on the grill!

Café Brûlot

4 SERVINGS

1	slice lemon peel		½	teaspoon vanilla
1	slice orange peel		½	cup brandy
2	cubes sugar		½	cup Grand Marnier™ (optional)
4-6	whole cloves		2	cups strong black coffee
1	(3 inch) stick cinnamon			

Place lemon peel, orange peel, sugar, cloves, cinnamon, vanilla, brandy and Grand Marnier™ in a chafing dish or frying pan. Warm to dissolve sugar. Ignite mixture in pan. Add coffee to extinguish flames. Serve in demitasse or thin footed mugs.

1963

The largest pretzel ever baked was created by Joseph Nacchio of Federal Baking, Philadelphia, PA. It weighed 40 pounds and was 5-feet across.

1730

Cheesecake was made popular at Philadelphia restaurants such as the "Cheesecake House" as early as the 1730s-1740s.

Wallis Warfield Simpson Cocktail · 1 DRINK

1	ounce gin	1	drop of blue food coloring
1	ounce Cointreau™	1	sugar rimmed Old Fashion glass
1	ounce fresh lime juice		ice

In a cocktail shaker, mix gin, Cointreau™ and lime juice. Add one drop of blue food color, which should turn the drink the color of the Duchess of Windsor's wedding dress! Pour into sugar rimmed Old Fashion glasses.

Sangría Delight · 12 SERVINGS

2	bottles of dry white wine (750 ml bottles)	1	lime, sliced
2	oranges, sliced	1	cup confectioners' sugar
1	lemon, sliced	⅓	cup brandy
			ice

In a pitcher, combine ingredients and stir until sugar is dissolved. Refrigerate overnight. Serve over ice in wine glasses. Garnish with some of the marinated fruit.

Foolproof Frozen Margaritas · 6-8 GENEROUS DRINKS

6	ounce can of frozen limeade		ice
6	ounces triple sec		salt
6	ounces tequila		

Empty frozen limeade into a blender. Use the empty can to measure triple sec and add to blender. Repeat for tequila. Add ice to fill the blender and blend on high speed until smooth. Salt the rim of the glass if desired and serve immediately.

City Tavern Eggnog

10-12 SERVINGS

7	large egg yolks	¾	cup bourbon
¾	cup granulated sugar	¾	cup Appleton Rum™
2	cups heavy cream	¼	cup brandy
1	cup whole milk		freshly grated nutmeg, for garnish

In the large bowl of an electric mixer, beat together the egg yolks and sugar on high speed for about 5 minutes, until thick and pale yellow. Gradually beat in the cream, milk, and bourbon, Appleton rum and brandy. Cover and refrigerate until completely chilled. Serve in cups or mugs. Garnish with nutmeg.

Reprinted with permission from *The City Tavern Cookbook: Recipes from the Birthplace of American Cuisine* ©2009 by Walter Staib.

Frozen Watermelon Daiquiri

4-6 DRINKS

Cut and freeze watermelon at least 6 hours ahead of serving time.

½	seedless watermelon, cut into 1 inch cubes then freeze in a freezer bag	1	tablespoon confectioners' sugar
¾-1 cup rum (not spiced)			handful of fresh mint leaves, chopped
			mint, for garnish

Put frozen watermelon cubes into blender. Add rum, confectioners' sugar and mint leaves. Blend (you may have to push watermelon down several times) until smooth. Pour into a daiquiri glass. Place mint sprig on top for garnish.

1913

A dinner invitation from a Jefferson Medical College Alumni Association event, circa 1913, describes the first part of the dinner party as consisting of "cigarettes and martinis". This was followed by appetizers and Jefferson Punch. Cigars and coffee followed dessert. While, the exact recipe for the Jeff Punch is unknown, this is our approximation.

Refreshing Gin Buck

1 DRINK

1½	ounces gin	4½	ounces ginger ale
	ice cubes		lime wedges, quartered

Pour gin into a highball glass filled ¾ with ice cubes. Add ginger ale. Squeeze juice of a quartered lime into drink and stir. Garnish with lime wedge on the edge of the glass.

Jefferson Punch

20 SERVINGS

½	fifth vodka	2	(3 ounce) cans frozen lemonade, thawed
½	pint Seagram's 7™ Blended Whiskey	2	(32 ounce) bottles ginger ale, chilled
1	(12 ounce) can frozen orange juice, thawed		

Pour ingredients into a large punch bowl. Stir gently. Serve over ice in punch cups.

Garnish with orange slices.

Pomegranate Martini

2 SERVINGS

1¾	cups pomegranate juice	1	cup ice
2	ounces Absolute Citron vodka or white tequila		splash of sparkling water, optional
1	ounce Cointreau liquor		squeeze of lemon, optional

Shake ingredients in a shaker and put in chilled martini glasses.

Frozen pomegranate fruit may be used as a garnish.

Bread and Butter Pickles

8	sliced cucumbers		1	teaspoon turmeric
2	cups sliced onions		1	teaspoon pickling spice tied in a bag
2	cups cider vinegar			
3	cups sugar			

Boil cucumbers and onions in salted water, let stand 3 hours. Drain and add cider vinegar, sugar, turmeric and pickling spice. Cook slowly until boils. Cool, spoon into canning jars and seal.

1876

Shane's Candies was founded at 2nd and Market Street and remains the oldest continuously operating purveyor of handmade chocolates in the U.S.

Margie's Watermelon Pickles

PICKLES

3	quarts watermelon rind, cut into cubes		3	cups water
¼	cup salt		1	cup cider vinegar

SYRUP

2	cups water		4	more cups sugar
2	cups sugar		3	drops cinnamon oil
2	cups cider vinegar		2	drops clove oil

Pickles: Trim watermelon rind from peel and the pink pulp. Sprinkle with salt and enough water to cover. Let soak for several hours or overnight. Drain. Cook until tender in 3 cups water and 1 cup vinegar. Drain well.
Syrup: Boil 2 cups water, sugar, and vinegar. Set aside overnight. Add 4 cups sugar, cinnamon and cloves. Add watermelon cubes and bring to boil. Pour into a crock and let stand overnight. Spoon into canning jars and seal.

Flavored Sugars (Vanilla, Cinnamon, or Cardamon)

MAKES 2 CUPS EACH

Makes an unique hostess gift when presented in a glass jar with a colorful label.

Start with 2 cups granulated white sugar:

VANILLA SUGAR

split a vanilla bean in half and scrape the seeds from the bean into the sugar

CINNAMON SUGAR

2 tablespoons ground Saigon cinnamon

2 cinnamon sticks, break in half and insert into jar of mixed sugar and ground cinnamon

CARDAMON SUGAR

½ cup green cardamom pods. Bury pods in sugar.

Prepare desired sugar flavor as above. Pour mixed sugar into an airtight glass jar (a canning jar works well). Apply appropriate label to jar.

Flavors last for a year or more.

Homemade Mosquito Repellant

MAKES 4 OUNCES

Adapted from The Rhythm of the Family: A Sense of Wonder Through the Seasons, (Roost Books, 2011), by Amanda Blake Soule and Stephen Soule

All natural way to avoid bug bites.

4 ounces witch hazel

¾ teaspoon eucalyptus oil

¾ teaspoon lemongrass oil

¾ teaspoon citronella oil

Pour ingredients in a 4 ounce spray bottle. Label bottle as insect repellent. Shake before each application.

Healthy Snack Ideas

- Toasted whole wheat pita instead of crackers. Cut pita into wedges, spray with olive oil and toast in oven at 350° for 3 minutes

- Use a combination of half yogurt and half salsa as a dip for vegetables

- Fresh fruit plus ¼ cup of nuts (be sure to measure nut serving)

- Eat pickles

- Olives – 8 to 10 serving size

- Reduced fat cheese (50 calories or less per ounce)

- Sugar free gelatin cups

- Edamame – lightly steamed or microwave with sea salt

- Raw shredded cabbage for nibbling or drizzle with a flavored balsamic vinegar

- Cherry tomatoes, raw or microwaved. Sprinkle with basil olive oil.

- Top vegetable slices (zucchini, squash, cucumber) with soy cheese slice and toast on whole wheat bread

Daily Calorie Distribution

CARBOHYDRATES

- Eat 20 to 40 grams of carbohydrate at breakfast
- 40 – 50% of daily calories should be carbohydrates
- Contain 4 calories per gram
- If you eat 1200 calories per day- 120 to 150 grams should come from carbohydrates
- If you eat 1500 calories per day- 150 to 190 grams should come from carbohydrates
- If you eat 1800 calories per day- 180 to 225 grams should come from carbohydrates
- Do not avoid eating carbohydrates at breakfast; you need a small amount

PROTEINS

- Eat 14 to 30 grams of protein at breakfast
- 15 to 20% of daily calories should be proteins
- Contain 4 calories per gram If you eat 1200 calories per day- 45 to 65 grams should come from proteins
- If you eat 1500 calories per day- 150 to 190 grams should come from proteins
- If you eat 1800 calories per day- 180 to 225 grams should come from proteins
- One ounce of animal fat contains 7 grams of protein
- Eat a protein with a carbohydrate

FATS

- 25 to 35% of daily calories may be fats
- Contain 9 calorie per gram
- If you eat 1200 calories per day- 35 to 47 grams should come from fats
- If you eat 1500 calories per day- 42 to 58 grams should come from fats
- If you eat 1800 calories per day- 50 to 70 grams should come from fats
- Choose monounsaturated fats. Avoid saturated, trans and polyunsaturated fats

Cooking Conversions and Bar Drink Measurements

COOKING MEASUREMENT CONVERSIONS

1 teaspoon = ⅙ fl. ounce

1 tablespoon = ½ fl. ounce

1 tablespoon = 3 teaspoons

1 dessert spoon (UK) = 2.4 teaspoons

16 tablespoons = 1 cup

12 tablespoons = ¾ cup

10 tablespoons + 2 teaspoons = ⅔ cup

8 tablespoons = ½ cup

6 tablespoons = ⅜ cup

5 tablespoons + 1 teaspoon = ⅓ cup

4 tablespoons = ¼ cup

2 tablespoons = ⅛ cup

2 tablespoons + 2 teaspoons = ⅙ cup

1 tablespoon = ¹⁄₁₆ cup

2 cups = 1 pint

2 pints = 1 quart

3 teaspoons = 1 tablespoon

48 teaspoons = 1 cup

1 cup = 8 fluid ounces

2 cups= 1 pint

2 cups= 16 fluid ounces

1 quart = 2 pints

4 cups = 1 quart

4 cups = 32 fluid ounces

8 cups = 4 pints

8 cups = ½ gallon

8 cups = 64 fluid ounces

4 quarts =1 gallon

4 quarts = 128 fluid ounces

1 gallon (gal) = 4 quarts

16 ounces = 1 pound

Pinch = Less than ⅛ teaspoon

IMPERIAL TO METRIC

¼ teaspoon = 1.25 ml

½ tsp = 2.5 ml

1 tsp = 5 ml

1 tablespoon = 15 ml

¼ cup = 60 ml

⅓ cup = 75 ml

½ cup = 125 ml

⅔ cup = 150 ml

¾ cup = 175 ml

1 cup = 250 ml

1⅛ cups = 275 ml

1¼ cups = 300 ml

1½ cups = 350 ml

1⅔ cups = 400 ml

1¾ cups = 450 ml

2 cups = 500 ml

2½ cups = 600 ml

3 cups = 750 ml

3⅔ cups = 900 ml

4 cups = 1 liter

WEIGHT CONVERSION

½ oz = 15g	8 oz = 250 g
1 oz = 25 g	9 oz = 275 g
2 oz = 50 g	10 oz = 300 g
3 oz = 75 g	12 oz = 350 g
4 oz = 100 g	1 lb = 500 g
6 oz = 175 g	1½ = 750 g
7 oz = 200 g	2 lb = 1 kg

BAR DRINK MEASUREMENTS

1 dash = 6 drops	1 std. whiskey glass = 2 ounces
3 teaspoons = ½ ounce	1 pint = 16 fluid ounces
1 pony = 1 ounce	1 fifth = 25.6 fluid ounces
1 jigger = 1 ½ ounce	1 quart = 32 fluid ounces
1 large jigger = 2 ounces	

CAKE PAN SIZE CONVERSIONS

20cm springform cake pan = 8 inch	23cm springform cake pan = 9 inch
20cm square cake pan = 8 inch	25cm springform cake pan = 10 inch

MEASUREMENT ABBREVIATIONS

tsp = teaspoon	gal = gallon
Tbsp = tablespoon	lb = pound
fl = fluid	sm = small
oz = ounce	lg = large
pkg = package	g = gram
c = cup	kg = Kilogram
pt = pint	ml =Milliliter
qt = quart	

Bibliography

Angelo, F. Michael, University Archivist and Special Collections Librarian for the Thomas Jefferson University, Philadelphia, Pennsylvania (provided access to original historical documents and photographs).

Bowers, Eloise. *History of the Women's Board of Thomas Jefferson Hospital.* 1987. Jefferson University Printing Center, Philadelphia, PA.

Bowers, Eloise. *History of the Women's Board of Thomas Jefferson Hospital, Second Supplement.* 1993. Jefferson University Printing Center, Philadelphia, PA.

Bowers, Eloise. *History of the Women's Board of Thomas Jefferson Hospital, Third Supplement.* 1996. Jefferson University Printing Center, Philadelphia, PA.

Briggs, Richard. *The New Art of Cookery, According to the Present Practice.1792.* W. Spotswood, R. Campbell, & B. Johnson Publishers, Philadelphia PA.

Bundy, Beverly. *The Century in Food: America's Fads and Favorites. 2002.* Collectors Press, Inc.

Jorgenson, Janice (Ed). "Philadelphia Brand Cream Cheese," *Encyclopedia of Consumer Brands. 1994.* Vol. 1: Consumable Products, 1994. St. James, Detroit, MI.

Lee Gabriel Hilde. *Taste of the States: A Food History of America. 1992.* Howell Press, Charlottesville, VA.

Pendergrast, Mark. *For God, Country and Coca-Cola. 1993.* Basic Books, ISBN: 0465054684.

Soule, Amanda Blake and Stephen Soule. *The Rhythm of the Family: A Sense of Wonder Through the Seasons,* 2011. Roost Books.

Trager, James L. *The Food Chronology: A Food Lover's Compendium of Events and Anecdotes, from Prehistory to the Present. 1997.* Owl Books, New York.

Wagner, Frederick & J. Woodrow Savacool. *Legend & Lore: Jefferson Medical College, 1996.* William T. Cooke, Publishing, Inc., Devon, P.A

Wagner, Frederick & J. Woodrow Savacool. *Chronological History and Alumni Directory: Annotated and Illustrated, 1824-1990. 1992.* Thomas Jefferson University, Philadelphia, PA.

Yeo, Theresa. *Personal Interviews with longtime Women's Board members: Mrs. Elinor Medoff, Dorrance Hamilton, Marcella Theodos, and Audrey Knowles, 2011-2012.*

Online Sources:

history.aspxhttp://online.wsj.com/article/SB123758172905298941.html

http://italianmarketphilly.org/experience-the-market/market-history/

http://en.wikipedia.org/wiki/Cuisine of Philadelphia

http://en.wikipedia.org/wiki/Tastykake

http://jeffline.jefferson.edu/Education/forum/00/02/articles/solis.html

http://libwww.library.phila.gov/CenCol/exhibitionfax.htm

http://ritasice.com/about-us/our-http://www.tjuhortho.org/history.html

http://slakethirst.com/2005/10/07/fish-house-punch/

http://www.amorosobaking.com/consumer/history.aspxhttp://www.bassettsicecream.com/historyhttp://www.danteandluigis.com/history.htm

http://www.justborn.com/get-to-know-us/our-historyhtmlhttp://www.readingterminalmarket.org/about/early

http://www.tastykake.com/aboutus/

http://www83.homepage.villanova.edu/richard.jacobs/FOOD/stromboli.htm

http://www.yuengling.com/our_story/

Index

1930s

The Philly Cheese Steak Sandwich, a Philadelphia classic, was developed quite by chance in the 1930s by Harry and Pat Olivieri as an alternative to the hot dog lunch. The sandwiches originally sold for 5 cents and were cheese-less. Cheese Whiz™ was added in the 1950s by an employee who wanted to liven up the sandwich. A cheese steak is more of a chipped steak than an actual steak and is served with or without onions.

Z

ZUCCHINI *(also see Squash)*

Philly Cheese Steak Sandwich

MAKES 3 HEARTY SANDWICHES

We almost forgot to include our Philly Cheese Steak recipe!

2   tablespoons vegetable oil

1   large sweet onion, chopped

1   pound thinly sliced rib-eye steak (preferred) or 1 pound deli roast beef, thinly sliced

    Cheese Whiz™ or 9 slices Provolone cheese or 9 slices American cheese

3   Italian long rolls, 10 to 12 inches

In a 12-inch frying skillet, heat oil over medium heat; add onions and cook, stirring, until soft. Push onions to side of pan. Add meat, continuously shredding and stirring until browned. Slice rolls horizontally. Place ⅓ of the cooked meat on each roll. Top with the cheese of your choice. Add onions, if desired. Salt and pepper to taste.

Optional additions to sandwich include: marinara sauce, sautéed mushrooms, or sautéed green, red, or yellow peppers.

The Thomas Jefferson University Hospital
Women's Board

925 Chestnut Street, Suite 110
Philadelphia, PA 19107

Please send me_____ copies of *At The Table, A Luscious Collection of Philadelphia's Favorite Recipes* at $29.95 per copy.

ALL ORDERS MUST BE PRE-PAID

(Make Checks or Money Order Payable to: TJUH Women's Board)

Amount of Order	$	_____
Shipping & Handling	$	8.00
Gift Wrap $1.00/copy	$	_____
Total Amount of Order	$	_____

Name: _____

Address: _____

City/State/Zip: _____

Daytime Phone: _____

Please allow 8-10 days for delivery.

To order online, visit our website at:
www.jeffersonhospital.org/womensboard/

Call (215) 955-6831 Monday through Friday
(9 AM to 4 PM) to order by phone.

The Thomas Jefferson University Hospital
Women's Board

925 Chestnut Street, Suite 110
Philadelphia, PA 19107

Please send me_____ copies of *At The Table, A Luscious Collection of Philadelphia's Favorite Recipes* at $29.95 per copy.

ALL ORDERS MUST BE PRE-PAID

(Make Checks or Money Order Payable to: TJUH Women's Board)

Amount of Order	$ _____
Shipping & Handling	$ 8.00
Gift Wrap $1.00/copy	$ _____
Total Amount of Order	$ _____

Name: _____

Address: _____

City/State/Zip: _____

Daytime Phone: _____

Please allow 8-10 days for delivery.

To order online, visit our website at:
www.jeffersonhospital.org/womensboard/

Call (215) 955-6831 Monday through Friday
(9 AM to 4 PM) to order by phone.